Marie Annie Henson

Echoes from the heart

Songs piped during the first year of manhood

Marie Annie Henson

Echoes from the heart
Songs piped during the first year of manhood

ISBN/EAN: 9783337265298

Printed in Europe, USA, Canada, Australia, Japan

Cover: Foto ©Thomas Meinert / pixelio.de

More available books at **www.hansebooks.com**

ECHOES FROM THE HEART.

SONGS PIPED DURING THE FIRST

YEAR OF MANHOOD

BY

ANDREW M. McCONNELL,

BIRMINGHAM, ALABAMA.

1895.

———————

ALABAMA EDITION.

———————

ATLANTA, GA.:
THE FOOTE & DAVIES CO., PRINTERS AND BINDERS.
1895.

Dedicated

With faithful
affection and esteem
to loved acquaintances and
literary friends, and to every person who
possesses a warm heart which pulsates with love
for Christ, for pure womanhood, for noble
manhood, and for the honor
of our glorious
Southland.

"*Most men know love but as a part of life;*
 They hide it in some corner of the breast,
 Even from themselves; and only when they rest
In the brief pauses of that daily strife,
Wherewith the world might else be not so rife,
 They draw it forth (as one draws forth a toy
 To soothe some ardent, kiss-exacting boy)
And hold it up to sister, child or wife.
Ah me! why may not love and life be one?
 Why walk we thus alone, when by our side,
 Love, like a visible God, might be our guide?
How would the marts grow noble! and the street,
Worn like a dungeon floor by weary feet,
See m then a golden court-way of the sun!"

—HENRY TIMROD.

CONTENTS.

vi   CONTENTS.

PART II.

PART III.

INTRODUCTORY.

Professor Andrew M. McConnell was born in Blount County, Alabama, April 22, 1873. The community was twenty miles from any railroad, on the Sand Mountain, one of the healthiest and prettiest rolling countries of the South. His father was a plain, unpretentious farmer who made no more than enough to supply his actual needs.

His early associates and surroundings were not conducive to intellectual growth, nor calculated to foster the spirit of high ambition which characterizes this sweet singer of the South, and which has served him for Herculean tasks.

As a child he describes himself as uncouth. He had no sister and only one brother, who was twenty years older than himself; therefore, he was mostly alone, communing with his thoughts and growing aspirations.

At eleven, he commenced attending three months schools; the rest of the year doing hard work on the farm. Trained with Puritan strictness, he joined the Methodist church at eight, and became a favorite with ministers, teachers and old people.

At school he could not bear to be excelled in study or play, and was graduated without a demerit. His insatiate love of knowledge led him to read everything he could get, and after a hard

2

day's work he would pore over books until late by a pine-knot light.

At fifteen, he attended, for four months, an academy in a village nine miles away, and was there advanced sufficiently to teach a country school, but was too young.

In 1890, at the age of seventeen, he was appointed census enumerator, and in the month saved one hundred dollars. With this and his father's assistance, he was enabled to attend Blount College one year. Next summer he taught a country school of seventy-five pupils in a distant part of the county; then returned to college, and in the coming June received the degree, B. S., gained the prize for the greatest improvement in penmanship, had held a high office in the military organization, and represented his society in commencement debate.

Next summer he commenced a three months school, but his failing health compelled him to give up the work. Later he obtained the principalship of the Jonesboro Academy, situated in that beautiful resident town, thirteen miles south of Birmingham. From an ordinary school of thirty or forty pupils, he built it up in three months to an enrollment of one hundred and three, including some boarders; continued a session; then taught some writing schools; then, a summer school in Etowah County.

Next September, 1894, he taught a school in the suburbs of the city of Bessemer, until Christ-

mas; then attended the Southern University at
Greensboro, and in five months completed a full
year's course, represented the Belles-lettres Society in commencement debate, and gained for it
the honors.

Last summer he traveled over a large portion
of his native State, met a number of writers,
educators and other distinguished persons; but
spent most of his time in writing and studying.

In the fall of 1894, he went to South Carolina
in order to learn more of the Southern States and
people, and accepted a position in the Blackville
High School.

As editor of the "Department of Southern Literature" in the *Southern Homestead Magazine*, Atlanta, Ga., he is doing a grand work.

At twenty-one, he was not known in the literary world; during the following year, besides
writing a number of prose articles for periodicals,
he has written two hundred and fifty pages of
poetry, studied theology, metaphysics, general
literature, and read extensively in Southern literature; also has taught eight months, has given a
course of biographical lectures, and has been an
associate editor of the *Southern Homestead Magazine;* notwithstanding his eyes, during half of the
year, would not admit of study at night.

Recently the young author, who never took a
drink of whisky, who never used tobacco in any
form, who never mingled with the giddy throng
of the ballroom, who never played cards, even

as a social game, and from whose lips a profane or indecent word was never heard to fall, was licensed to preach by the Methodist Episcopal Church, South.

The keys to his success, he gives in these four mottoes: "Where there is a will, there is a way;" "They can conquer, who but think they can;" "Man grows, as higher grows his aims;" and "*What others can do, I can do.*"

Comment is unnecessary. The bare facts tell the story of struggling genius, indefatigable energy, and unconquerable ambition. This volume of embryonic efforts, he designs not for the literary world, but for the people who would appreciate songs from one of their own ways; yet these, the verses of his boyhood, we feel to be but a faint prelude to the flood of music that will some day pour forth from the ripened soul of this poet of the South.

MARIE ANNIE HENSON.

FORK UNION, VIRGINIA, June, 1895.

ECHOES FROM THE HEART.

There are echoes of music from Dreamland,
　And whispers from Fancy's retreat;
They are sweet as home songs in the evening,
　Which the ears of the wanderer meet.

There are echoes from voices in childhood,
　In the merriest tones we have heard,
And they render our soul ever joyous,
　As the notes from a jubilant bird.

There are echoes from loved ones, departed,
　Who have traveled a different way:
They are sung in the tenderest sadness
　On the flutes for sweet Memory's lay.

There are echoes of songs from a dear one,
　And the whispers of love, with its kiss;
Not a tongue can express their sweet soothing,
　Nor a pen e'er reveal their wild bliss.

Thus the heart ever echoes a music
　Of a soft and enlivening sound,
It is laden with happiest feelings,
　That a lonely, sad life ever found!

THE WISH OF MY HEART.

Oh! could you only tell me,
  With those sweet brown eyes of yours,
That some day you may love me
  With the love that e'er endures;

My days would be far brighter—
  All the stars would shine above;
I'd mount the rounds of greatness,
  If supported by your love.

And could you only trust me
  With your hand and with your heart,
I'd pray for God to bless me,
  With the honor due my part.

Michael Angelo was once asked to fashion a statue out of snow. Think of such a peerless genius spending his invaluable time upon a foible of fancy, which for its existence, depended upon the fluctuations of temperature! Just so foolish is it, for gifted minds to contribute the supreme efforts of their evanescent years, to appease the fickle whims of reputation. All whose memories are less ephemeral than their years, have painted the incarnation of illustrious deeds and thoughts upon the eternal and unsullied canvas of exalted character.

VIVIAN.

When the morning sun is rising,
  Robed in silvery beams of white,
And so gently is baptizing
  All the land with floods of light;
When the dew is disappearing,
  And its rainbows we can see;
Then my mind is sweetly nearing,
  Vivian, fair, with thoughts of thee!

When the sun in noonday splendor,
  Rides upon his flames of fire,
And his rays so warm and tender
  Clothe the earth in green attire;
When mankind are happy drinking
  Nature's waters; cool, and free;
I am then so happy thinking,
  Vivian, sweetest one, of thee!

When the sun is calmly pacing
  Down his western streets of gold,
And the evening skies embracing
  All his parting smiles, to hold;
When these beams, in sweet resplendence,
  Are reflected o'er the lea;
Then I think, with fond remembrance,
  Vivian, loveliest one, of thee!

When the evening shadows hover,
  And the stars in heav'n are found;
When the darkness all things cover—
  Laborers, tired, go, homeward bound;

Then my heart is filled with sadness,
　Hope, the only star for me,
Shines to fill my soul with gladness,
　Vivian, noblest one, 'tis thee!

When the hours in study fleeting,
　Fill my lamp with midnight oil,
· And I seek from Sleep a greeting—
　Shunning all my mental toil;
First I kneel in secret prayer,
　Asking blessings full and free—
All the Savior's tenderest care,
　Vivian, purest one, for thee!

Then when I am sweetly dreaming
　Of fair Future's angel prize,
All I see in Fancy beaming,
　Are your tender sweet brown eyes;
All the bliss in Dreamland's glory—
　All the hope it has for me—
Future's home will tell the story,
　Vivian, dearest one, with thee!

————————

There's not a pain that lives in sorrow—
　No thought that born with tear,
But what will be a joy to-morrow—
　A smile so sweet and dear.

GREENSBORO.

Far down the sunny side of "Here we rest,"
There blooms a Southern town by nature blest
    With beauties rare, to love and please;
Sequestered round with shrub and spreading oak,
Its lovely homes are wrapped in Verdure's cloak,
    Which kindly hails the sylvan breeze.

Fair lawns imprison Beauty in her prime;
Their shades o'erlook vied Pleasure's hidden mine,
    Enchantment lends a brighter view—
What venerable, stately buildings grand!
Where oft I know, have gentle zephyrs fanned,
    For grief, a long, farewell adieu.

Fair Erin's wit, old England's pride, nor Spain,
Could ne'er for lovelier girls, and sweet, make claim,
    Than those who grace our Southern land.
From broad Kentucky's blue grass fields of green
To Florida's coronal golden sheen
    That decks the face of glowing sand,

There's not another town more richly blest,
With lovely happy homes, with men the best,
Than this fair model town of Greensboro.
Sweet Spring, in virgin prime, from Winter's snow,
And all his chilling rain and dew,

Now hides in hearts of Japonicas red,
And mirrors the sweet smiles of May long dead.
But Spring, a sweeter, lovelier home than this,
Hath dedicated to vied Beauty's throne—
This throne is sacred to the girls alone,
Whose smiles e'er bring Greensboro's bliss.

———

Hallowed love, with peace of mind swings ajar
the golden gates of Eden, opening into earthly
Paradise.

———

The earthly abode of happiness is in the halls of
activity—never content to dwell in the house of
idleness.

———

SORROW'S MIDNIGHT THOUGHTS.

The night is cold and dark and dreary,
  The rain is falling fast;
And so my life is dark and sad and weary
  With rain and storm and blast.

It seems sweet Sleep no more is coming,
  My tear-drenched eyes to close,
The rain still beats its plaintive humming,
  My heart with grief o'erflows.

Oh! mother! mother, dear! what's giving
   My heart this bleeding sore?
Oh! has she left this world of living?
   She's gone forevermore!

Where is the lovely face of mother,
   The wrinkled hands and brow?
Oh! never can I love another,
   As I love mother now!

The hands that cared for me are moulding
   And turning back to clay;
The arms that held me oft, are folding,
   In death's lone silent way.

The lips that kissed me oft are going
   To leave no more imprint;
The heart that loved me long is showing,
   That life's sweet chord is rent.

My loving mother has departed
   Far from this world of care,
My tender soul is broken-hearted
   With grief I cannot bear.

O God! send Thy comforting Saviour,
   To guide my footsteps here,
So that I'll meet in heavenly favor,
   My sainted mother dear!

MY STAR OF HOPE.

In the happy realms of Fancy,
　There in peaceful skies of blue,
Shines my star of Hope so sweetly,
　That no other star I view.

Many nights, it's lovely shining
　Has so filled my heart with light,
That the night-time seems more lovely
　Than the day with sun so bright.

When I first its rays saw streaming
　To my lonely, saddened heart,
All my skies shone brightly beaming—
　All the darkness did depart.

Ah! what beauty then was filling
　All the glory in the blue;
Lonely cares it then was killing,
　And my Guiding Star I knew.

Then I dropped my cares and climbing
　Up the long and weary steep,
Sweetly did my Star keep timing
　With its twinkling to my feet.

Calmly breezes then were blowing,
　Laden with a blissful peace;
Happy flowers there were growing,
　Lovelier than the Golden Fleece.

Onward up the rising mountain,
   Nothing but my Star to lead!
Drinking at each clear cool fountain,
   Nothing but my Star to heed!

Soon strong wings, to me, were given,
   Swiftly to my Star I flew;
Oh! it was a happy heaven,
   Then to meet it in the blue.

We had met before—no never,
   But my heart said 'twould not do
From that time, till death, to sever,
   From my soul, the Star in blue.

Long we wandered mid the glory
   Of cerulean joys so free—
Happier than heroes of story,
   Ever found Fruition's lea.

Still more sweets were e'er unfolding
   To my rapture-stricken gaze—
Still my Star is kindly holding
   All the hope of earthly days.

Star of Hope! 'tis thou, in splendor,
   Queenly rules two castles grand;
And thy heart, supremely tender,
   Scatters sunshine o'er the land.

Literature's castle lightening
All earth's care, to give it love;
Art's fair temple ever brightening,
With the beauties from above.

These two temples in fair Aidenn,
Thou art evermore their queen;
And when death shall bring thee laden
With the richest harvest seen,

Oh! then I'll praise the God of heaven,
Who kindly gave our Southern sky,
The brightest star that could be given—
A jewel from an angel's eye.

The golden beams my Star sent flowing,
All through my warm and tender soul,
Then filled my life with purest glowing,
And ever through my heart will roll

A music sweet with heavenly beauty—
The noblest songs of God and love—
An aim to work and do my duty
And store my treasures all above.

So sweetly, through Elysium gliding
With thee, my Guiding Star of hope,
A nameless longing, life abiding,
With thee to go adown life's slope.

Oh, Duty! cruel, good, both blending,
    Conspired to part me from my Star;
Oh parting pain! what grief so rending!
    When time and distance did debar?

Youthful visions long unfolding,
    All life's beauties sweet and fair,
Faintly seemed a phantom, rolling
    To my Star of beauty rare.

Sweet Angel, since my childhood dreaming
    Of blissful joys in Fancy born,
Ambition points, with glorious beaming,
    A Star of Hope my heart to adorn.

I trusted God, fore'er believing
    His hand, some day, would kindly guide
To one congenial, e'er achieving,
    To stand in love close by my side.

A voice, it seemed, so gently told me,
    When first I gladly read your book,
You were my Guiding Star to hold me,
    Since then my hope can't help but look

To you, dear one, from all the living,
    To be my only Love so true;
For more of joy to me you're giving,
    Than all the rest of earth can do.

I could not think that Fate intended
   To give such honor to my part,
But still you say our souls are blended,
   And that you love me from your heart;

When I have nothing for your liking—
   No work commending for my name,
While others, talented, striking,
   And who have won a lasting fame,

Quite oft, to you, their love, have plighted,
   And longed to ever live for you,
Have had their fondest hopes e'er blighted,
   And lost the poise of manhood's due.

And still you gave to me'love's greeting,
   To others, ne'er you'd faintly shown,
And that just after our first meeting—
   Oh! has it not God's pointing shown?

I think fair Favor's envied smiling,
   And many talents just and true,
Good Heaven will give me for my whiling,
   Until I'm worthy, Love, of you.

I look for Fortune's kind caresses,
   And lovely music from above,
As long as God so richly blesses
   Me with your warm and tender love.

How could He now be but alluring
  With hopes that I can never gain?
Oh! could He leave without assuring,
  That soon, the goal, I may attain?

No Fate can never sadly sever,
  For aye, the souls that now are twin.
We can't be haunted long with "Never,"
  We cannot bear: "It might have been."

But as this life is not for pleasure,
  Nor all our work for selfish gain,
If duty take from me my treasure,
  I'll bravely bear the rending pain.

For duty, would my face be smiling,
  For you, my heart would bear its tear;
For God, my hours, I'd e'er be whiling,
  For you, my memory would be dear.

And if in love, you give another,
  The lovely hand that lay in mine;
In me you'll have a darling brother—
  A brother's love will still be thine.

But if for any reasons, other
  Than love then found sincerely true,
You give your hand then to another,
  But still love me till life be through.

Oh! in sorrow would be blighted,
  All the peace of life for me!
All my days would seem blighted
  With the gloom of misery!

I'd be alone in troubles sailing
  O'er my life's dread wasteful main;
The winds would howl a plaintive wailing—
  Death would be a happy pain.

For us to love, and ne'er united,
  Have to leave from life its bliss,
Would cause me, if by sin benighted,
  Soon to end my days in this.

But when the friends of earth forsake me,
  And my loved one turns to go,
Oh! then my God will kindly take me,
  Far from this sad world of woe!

But let us never look for sorrows,
  And pine o'er all expected woe;
But live in hope of bright to-morrows,
  And gather smiles while on we go.

"Ah, well! for us" one "sweet hope lies,
  Deeply buried from human eyes;
And in the future, angels may
  Roll the stone, from its grave away."

Your angel smiles embody a sun that makes
my heart bloom with many sweet, fragrant
roses of tender love.

Smiles re-echo the music of the soul.

AWAY FROM THEE.

How can I spend these lonely hours—
How can life's blessings fall in showers,
        Away from thee?

How can I hear the bird's sweet singing,
How can I feel the joys now springing,
        Away from thee?

How can I hunt, with friends, for pleasure,
How can I count long hours a treasure,
        Away from thee?

How can my days be blest of Heaven,
How can I work to spread life's leaven,
        Away from thee?

How can I wait our next sweet meeting,
And live so long without love's greeting,
        Away from thee?

My mind is dull but e'er reflecting
Of all the joys I'm not expecting,
        Away from thee?

My days are many, long, and dreary—
My heart is sad and lone and weary,
Away from thee!

I'll tell thee how I'll spend each hour,
For which, I pray God's strongest power,
While away from thee.

Until our meeting's lonely lateness,
I'll work to do all deeds of greatness,
While away from thee.

I'll strive to mark, like those of story,
My life, with acts for Honor's glory,
While away from thee.

I'll hunt for all life's peaceful beauty,
I'll try to do each coming duty,
While away from thee.

I'll pray for thee in secret prayer,
I'll ask for us His tenderest care,
While away from thee.

For thee, I'll soar to Fancy's Aidenn,
That all my songs be music laden,
While away from thee.

I'll tune my soul to beauties beaming,
With brightness only known to seeming,
While away from thee.

I'll show my pen the paths, though olden,
That lead the mind to thoughts still golden,
          While away from thee.

I'll wear a smile for duty's calling,
And think of thee, whate'er's befalling,
          While away from thee.

So when that happy hour of meeting
Arrives, at last,to bring love's greeting,
          When I meet with thee.

For all my work at God's commanding,
I'll be of high and noble standing,
          Worthy, Love, of thee!

THE LITTLE WORLD OF LOVE.

There's a little sweet world,
   With a king and a queen—
'Tis the happiest world
   That earth's mortals have seen.

'Tis the land of True Love,
   With its flowers so sweet;
It was sent from above,
   For the lover's retreat.

'Tis the home of the Spring
   And the beauties of May,
Where the birds ever sing
   All the sadness away.

There the heart is the sun,
  With a tender soft light,
And love's moon has been won,
  For the glory of night.

'Tis a land by the sea,
  With the river of Joy;
Where the Pleasures are free,
  And no woes can annoy.

'Tis the home of Content,
  Where she dwells all the while,
And her blessings are sent
  In a peaceful, sweet smile.

There a breeze gently blows
  From the haven of bliss,
And there nobody knows,
  When love's stealing a kiss.

'Tis a world for just two—
  Its rich king and fair queen;
They are strolling it through,
  While they're living a dream.

Many live there alone,
  Just to list to the sigh
Of sad Memory's moan
  For the dead, sleeping nigh.

Many pine in its shade
  O'er a heart rent in twain,
By a traitor betrayed,
  After hope had been slain.

Many live there for life
  Mid its bountiful bliss,
Far away from the strife
  And the trouble of this.

'Tis a little sweet world,
  With a king and a queen;
'Tis the happiest world
  That earth's mortals have seen.

A life without love is like a violin without a
bow to awaken the music.

STREAMS OF SORROW.

Every heart has a trouble,
  And an unknown woe,
Where the lonely, cold rivers
  Of grief ever flow.

'Tis a wail from the desert
  Of a wasted life,
Or a groan o'er the failures
  In a hopeless strife.

Weary man born of sorrows,
  There is yet a balm—
In the happy to-morrows,
  Many days of calm.

Breathe a prayer in the evening
  From that heart of thine,
Praying blessing of Heaven
  Evermore to shine.

There is balm in sweet Gilead
  And a peace thine own;
There is glory in living
  When the clouds have flown.

SETTING SUN.

There's a bright and golden glory
  Round the setting of sun,
And a soft tender radiance
  From its flushings have come.

So when life's sun is setting,
  May effulgence remain
Of a fair golden splendor,
  From a life without stain!

May it fall in tenderness
  O'er the hearts that I love;
May it point them to Heaven,
  And beckon them above.

MY LOST LORENE.

In a lone valley rise, my dear one lies
'Neath the flowers that sigh round her tomb.
And the willow trees weep in mournful sleep
For the love and the joy of life's bloom.

CHORUS.

Oh! my darling Lorene never more is seen,
Since we laid her to rest in the grave.
And my joys ever seem still to haunt the stream,
And to weep o'er her dear lonely grave.

Many years now have past since I saw her last,
Still I list to the strains of regret;
For a dreariness sways all the burdensome days,
Since the star of my hope has been set.

But in Heaven above I shall meet my Love,
And we never shall part any more.
She will greet with a kiss at the gates of bliss!
And we'll live there to love as before!

———————

This heart of mine has culled from the murmer-
ings of streams, the songs of birds, the fragrance
of flowers, the whispers of fancy, the longings of
childhood, the musings of Dreamland and the
echoes of hope, a garland of tender words for
love's dictionary, which at every touch of the
pen, like a kaleidoscope, it presents a new and
varied picture of the beautiful queen of my affec-
tions.

OUR HOME.

We'll have a home, somewhere, sometime,
  My darling Love and I ;
Where happy days will sweetly chime
  In music as they die.
The future years of love and rhyme
  Will kiss and pass on by.

Perhaps 'twill be a cottage neat,
  Where want has bid farewell,
Upon a cosy lawn retreat,
  Where Love has come to dwell.
And everything be fair and sweet,
  Beyond what words can tell.

Perchance in noisy city's din—
  But be it where it may,
A quiet peace will reign within,
  Where Love and I shall stay.
Content and joy we'll kindly win,
  And keep them every day.

That home may be an Aidenn shore.
  Beyond life's sunset glare,
In lovely Eden's garden store,
  'Mid beauties sweet and rare :
Somewhere, sometime, we'll part no more !
  Then love's vied bliss we'll share !

THE LOVERS' SONG.

We don't know what the future brings,
    We'll only love and wait,
And fly with hope, on viewless wings,
    To lovely Eden's gate.

We know our hearts were made to love,
    And taught to e'er be true;
We know our souls will join above,
    When parting pain is through!

But can't sweet Hymen for us join
    Our hands and hearts while here,
A music sweet of union born
    Would soothe each coming year.

We don't know what Hereafter gives,
    We'll hope it's only bliss—
A home where love in fondness lives,
    And Heaven sends its kiss.

"WHEN LOOKS ARE FOND AND WORDS ARE FEW."

No words are coined that can reveal
The happiness which lovers feel,
While hearts are learning to be true—
"When looks are fond and words are few."

They seek the lone sequestered spot
Where blooms the sweet forget-me-not;
Then, falls love's peace with evening dew,
"When looks are fond and words are few."

Then, strolling home by Luna's light,
They feel a joy beyond delight,
While stars are peeping through the blue,
And "looks are fond and words are few!"

They sip from future's cup its bliss,
And find a heav'n in every kiss,
An feel enraptured, through and through,
"When looks are fond and words are few!"

They sail for earth's enchanted isle,
Where Peace and Love forever smile,
There Paradise they still renew,
"When looks are fond and words are few!"

THE HAND OF GOD.

I was born in Poverty's dry vale,
    Bred to work and bear the sun;
But no man is doomed to work and fail,
    Better climes, I since have won—
        'Twas the hand of God!

Days have filled themselves with dread despair,
    Bringing nothing but sad gloom,
Times have borne me cares too hard to bear,
    Still the springtime came with bloom.
        'Twas the hand of God.

Many times I've fallen helpless, faint,
  Struggling hard up learning's hill;
But the goal ne'er smiled to greet complaint,
  Birth was given to my will!
    'Twas the hand of God.

TWILIGHT WHISPERS.

The evening breezes stir
  A sweet but plaintive murmur—
The whispers borne from her
  Who holds my heart in bondage.

A soothing calm they give
  Of tender peace and quiet;
They ask me should I live
  Forever 'way from Lula!

Their gentle sighs repeat
  The echoes low and cheering,
Of words in answered greet
  To love made known at twilight.

Mild zephyrs, bear a word
  From me to distant Lula;
It fell from Hymen's bird,
  Which sings of blissful union:

Remind her of the day,
  Still bound in fairy future,
The first of tranquil May,
  When we shall enter Eden!

THE BLUES.

Long dreary days of burdened gloom,
Oft wilt awhile life's fragrant bloom ;
Ah! would a gentle hand then choose
To fondly pet away the blues.

My spirit sinks to dread despair,
And moans o'er heavy cares to bear;
Life's sweetening peace withholds its dues,
Without a hand to soothe the blues.

When hopeless failures end the day,
And dreariness beclouds my way,
To grief I bear the dreaded news,
Without loved hands to calm the blues.

A gentle, tender, maiden hand,
Resigned for life to love's command,
Would bring the balm Content renews,
By fondling off the dreaded blues.

There is a sacredly sweet pleasure and a timely
exercise of virtue in supporting each other, like
the cedars of Lebanon, till across the treacherous
quicksands between worthy effort and liberal
recognition.

MEMORIAL TO AN AGED MAN.

Buried is my father, loved so dearly!
  Buried with my joy, beneath the rose.
Time has made his weary feet to falter,
  And into the stream of Death he goes.
Many weary years of humble labor,
    Came and found him toiling for the right;
      Valiantly he led the Christian vanguard,
      Conquering all with Christ's sweet love and light.

Kindly trained he me, in early childhood,
  Guided all my steps with loving care,
Never uttered he a word of scolding—
  Love, that winning law, so good and rare,
Swayed he all in meek and kind obeyance.
    Now his form grows young in vernal May,
    Over life's tempestuous murky billows,
      Where he lives in Heaven's eternal day.

Never longed he for life's fame and honor,
  Only cared to walk the humble way.
Winters long of earthly cold and worry,
  Came to bleach his hair a silvery gray;
Sixty-seven springs, robed in their flowers,
    Filled his heart with gentleness and love;
And as many autumns, with their harvests,
    Garnered he life's golden grain above.

E'er the angel, Death, came with his summons,
  God had caused his time-worn feet to rest—
Paralyzed, they lay in quiet stillness,
    Resting calm to walk the regions blest.

Sweet repose, before the farewell parting !
Sunset radiance shone in golden tints,
Flushing splendors from a life of virtue,
Leaving in our hearts his kind imprints.

Time, that restless, swift, and turbid river,
Bore his spirit from its house of clay
To that Aidenn home so bright and vernal,
Perennial with the treasured sweets ot May.
Sands of earth oft glitter with rich jewels,
But our God sends Time and Death to store,
And to bear them to that Sweet Beyond,
Where they'll shine in crowns forevermore.

ACROSTIC TO L. N. S.

Lula, name that sounds still sweeter
Unto me each time I see
Lovely curls and shining tresses,
And her smile my love's beguile.

Never can my heart, hereafter,
E'en, forget the times I met
Lula's fond glad smile of welcome.
Sweetest peace will'never cease
Over memory land to hover,
'Newing thrills her music wills.

So as years roll in the future,
And perchance, if Fate's romance
Name a farewell day of parting,
Drown the hope that lives in longing,
Even the lays of loving days,
Round my heart will twine a pleasure,
Such as came with Lula's name!

TO MY AFFINITY.

It is not doubting thy sincerity,
   That gives my eye its frequent tear;
But it is Fate's unkind severity,
   Which never brings thy presence near.

I never fear—thy looks were lying,
   But 'twixt us are full many miles,
Which make my life continued dying,
   Deprived of thy angelic smiles!

'Tis not despair— thy love decaying,
   That robs each day of all that's sweet;
But 'tis the long—too long! delaying
   Of Heaven on earth—*When we shall meet!*

The roses of love beautify the garden of life.

TO LOUISE.

Your tender eyes of blue
Which sparkle like the dew
And whisper you are true,
My poise of heart annoy,
And all my thoughts decoy.

Your lovely rosy face,
Enhanced with nameless grace—
The model of our race,
'Tis this that I admire,
Enkindling love-lit fire!

Your sweet delicious lips,
Where love its nectar slips,
And bliss its sweetness sips!—
I live a painful sigh,
Debarred from Heaven so nigh!

Your wealth of raven hair
And bordering curls so fair
Entraps a beauty rare,
And charm my heart to tell
Louise, I love you well!

And when you sweetly sing,
Emotions tender spring
And bear me on the wing
Above life's care and strife
Into a happier life.

Your nobleness and pride
And virtues that abide,
Which angels could not chide,
Enthrone you as the shrine
To woo this heart of mine!

TRANSPORTED THOUGHTS.

Sweet emotions unknown to the tongue of ex-
pression,
Oft enkindle their fires on the hearth of the heart;
And our thoughts, their bright sparks, fly upward
and vanish,
Only seem to regret that they rose to depart.
Like a child, we will grasp at their brightness,
and wonder
That a beauty so rare was permitted to die.
Ne'er are words so transparent as to minor their
image;
Nevermore they return; we bemoan with a sigh!

Oh, the embers which sparkle in splendor and vanish
As they rise to a height where no mortal has been!
They are sighs from the Finite, enslaved, craving
freedom
In the realms of Infinity, beyond our ken.
Aspirations too pure not to rise toward Heaven,
And refuse to decay with the treasures of Time.
When they pass from our sight, I imagine bright
angels
Sweetly sing these soul songs to a music divine!

ACROSTIC.

How sweetly lives the year now dead!
Ah! blest its spring wherein our souls were wed!
Preserve for love this hallowed year just fled,
Pour Memory's incense round its sacred June,
Youth's heaven of love then ope'd life's fragrant
bloom.

Bright springs, with twenty wreaths of flowers
Intrusted thee their beauties—winsome powers!
Rich summers twenty times dissolved in thee,
Their sweet quintescent gentleness and glee;
How grand the gift of twenty autumn dyes!
Dear wealth of harvest hue they gave thy eyes;
As oft, cold winter snows, thy heart ne'er chilled,
Yet into it their purity instilled.

This year, may Heaven send its joys as free,
O Love! as when I found earth's heaven in thee!

My thoughts rob every moment of its tear—
You know each brings our meeting still more
near!

Love whispers Hope's consoling, soothing peace:
Our severed heart-aches some sweet day will cease.
Void life, were hearts not free to choose their
mates,
Enslaved, oh, hell! to take the will of Fates!

MY ANGEL.

There's an angel 'mong us earthlings,
    Come to glad the hearts of men;
And my only sad misgiving—
    Do you chide me with a sin?—
Is, I love her far too dearly,
    Wishing, hoping her my own.
In my mind she lives so nearly,
    Thoughts of others long have flown.

"Angel?" yes, for none are purer,
    Sent by God to fallen men,
Making hopes of Heaven surer,
    Smiling off the thoughts of sin.
Heaven's gentleness residing
    In her tender, virgin heart,
Beaming through her eyes, confiding,
    All the sweetness looks impart.

Eyes that show the soul's deep beauty,
    Wield an influence most divine;
And her heart's resigned to duty—
    Angel, to this life of mine!
None can know her but to love her,
    None can name her but to praise,
Zephyrs play my heart-song 'bove her:
    "Wondrous are her works and ways!"

Heaven wills each man an angel,
    Just to calm his troubled life;
Such a sacred, pure evangel,
    Is his loving, trusting wife.

But if Fate, so heartless, cruel,
   Chains him from his angel love,
He ne'er finds another jewel,
   Fit to lure his soul above.

So the angel God intended
   For my life, my heart has found;
Sweet to know my wanderings ended,
   And to feel our souls are bound.

But a feeling worse than sadness,
   Stays to haunt me with its pain,
Only hope can whisper gladness—
   'Twixt us intervenes a plain!
Months will pass before our meeting,
   Heals the wounds of long good-bye.
Love will keep the hours from fleeting,
   Loading each one with a sigh!

Dear friend, I wish you all the smile
   Fair future holds in store;
And trust you'll live in hearts not vile
   When you are here no more.

I gaze at my star of Hope, through a shower of
wishful tears and see glimmering tints of a rainbow
of promise. Unending thanks to Fate if he will
brighten the bow.

MY WATCH.

Many brag of their watches
　　Keeping times to the spheres;
And to hear them tell it,
　　They don't vary in years.

But my watch is as different
　　As a mule from a sheep;
It believes in changing,
　　No monotony to keep.

When I call on my sweetheart,
　　On the weather to chat,
My wild watch runs faster
　　Than a frightened stray cat.

When my girl is a-singing
　　A love song, just for me,
Every minute hops quicker,
　　Than an Alabama flea.

When her mother keeps sitting
　　In the parlor with us,
Till I have to leave her
　　Without getting a buss,

Then my watch runs slower,
　　Like a pull up the grade,
And I never felt "worser,"
　　Since the day I was made.

When she tells me she loves me
And is glad when I come;
Till next time, my watch slumbers,
Like a nig in the sun.

I have known it to vary,
Six long hours in a day;
It'll gain three when I am with her,
And lose three when away.

LORENE.

'Tis the home of my youth, and I love it so well:
There I roamed with Lorene o'er the hills and the
dells;
We would chase butterflies and we'd hunt for
birds' nests,
While we list to the singing of Robin-red-breast.

CHORUS.
Gone, those days with my love and my darling
Lorene;
I am living the past—all my joys are a dream
Of those happy spring days, and the sweet little
girl,
With a smiling, bright face and a long, golden curl!

We would gather wild flow'rs as we strolled
down the way
To the river, and wandered the rest of the day
Long the shore, watching fish, as we played in
the sand;
But as sun would go down, we went home, hand
in hand.

Soon sad death tore my heart from my darling
Lorene,
And she went to that land which we never have
seen,
But returns every night for my vigils to keep,
While I slumber and dream in my peaceful sweet
sleep!

COME BACK AGAIN.

(Song.)

Come once more, my wayward lover,
  Bring again your sweetest smile,
As you did in days long ended,
  When your heart was free from guile.
Walk with me in dreamy woodlands
  Where the quiet zephyrs blow;
Sing again, ye birds, as sweetly
  As the birds we used to know!

Wander with me to the willow
  Standing on a rising knoll;
Sing again sweet love songs tender,
  Breathing peace all through my soul;
Call me still your "little darling,"
  As you did once long ago;
Look again love's tender feeling,
  Which would send a heavenly glow!

Tell your love in happy fondness,
  Fold your trusting arms around,
Draw me to your noble bosom,
  Kiss each smile that can be found;
Bring again those pleasures golden,
  Love me as you used to do—
Bring, once more, the blisses olden,
  Tell me that you will be true!

WANTED A BETTER WORD.

Give me a word, Oh thou sweet singing bird,
  Plucked from the roses that bloom in the heart,
Borne by a dove from its garden of love,
  That to my dearest fair one will impart—

Feeling untold, that my heart cannot hold!
  Love is too weak to express its sweet bliss.
Can it be found with such musical sound,
  As to reveal the vied sweets of her kiss?

EYES.

I love the modest, brown-eyed girls
With golden hair and auburn curls,
Whose eyes entrap the autumn hue,
Reflected through the harvest dew.'

I love the gentle blue-eyed girls
 With shining hair and raven curls,
Whose eyes have stolen azure blue
From nights of moonless summer view.

The sweet brown eyes reveal a soul
And heart of purest, lasting gold;
A lovely grace, and beauty rare
Is hid in orbs so sweetly fair.

Oh, tender eyes of heavenly blue!
They show a heart that's kind and true;
They beam with virtue's angel smile,
And ne'er will trusting ones beguile.

HIGHER, LET ME CLIMB.

I'm broken-hearted, sad, and weary here,
Oppressed with toil and common fretful care;
There's nothing round me but a pressing crowd,
Unknown I sigh beneath life's shadowed shroud.

I'm tired of this dark, slippery, narrow dell,
Where heartless, wretched millions round me dwell;
Ah! can it be mad Fate's unchanging will
To bury me at foot of Honor's hill?

My heart is burning with ambition's fire,
My soul now craves to fly to regions higher,
Where live in manly prime the good and great
In happy homes in Manhood's grand estate.

Oh! have I power to mount and climb
The snow-capped mountains of my restless time?
Will feet and hands and will and muscle bring
The strength to reach life's cool refreshing spring?

Ye favored few, who live in Guerdon sweet,
Oh! come and help me climb this rocky steep;
But if you can't, then give a welcome smile,
'Twill bring me rest and courage all the while.

God help me reach that genius-gifted height
Where thoughts e'er shine with Heavenly light,
To brighten long, this dark, benighted place,
Where walk the unlearned sons of Adam's race.

Make haste, my soul! Life's rising morning sun
Is flying fast; his course will soon be run;
And strive to leave some act or thought sublime,
To better fallen man and conquer time.

———

I'll hold a prayer and a thought for thee—
One thought as long as the time shall be,
'Till work is done and I'm duty free,
Ah! then you'll see a fond smile and me!

UNKNOWN POEMS.

Every heart has some beautiful poems
  With a musical rhythm and rhyme,
Never sung to the pen but in mocking,
  But the soul feels their sweetness of chime.

There is one, a smooth song of the river,
  With a chorus of love very sweet;
There the trust of a heart was once given,
  And was sealed in that kissing retreat.

There are streams of the loneliest wailing—
  The refrains of the dying and dead,
With a chorus of the sweet Remember,
  In the tones of the hope that has fled.

But the poem that's sweetest and dearest,
  Is the chiming of golden soft bells;
With the rhyming of lovers' fond union,
  And the rhythm of Eden it swells!

———————

The old Latin maxim, "They can conquer who
but think they can," is an aphoristic embodiment
of my soul's most steadfast belief. And I will
conquer or prove false the motto: "Where there
is a will, there is a way," which has piloted every
illustrious seaman safely across the tempestuous
sea of life's endless endeavor, to earth's haven of
immortal memory and into Heaven's still harbor
of eternal felicity.

LORENE.

While musing through a happy lovelit dream,
I heard an angel's whisper breathe, "Lorene."

A blissful stillness calmed my restless soul,
And soothing peace did o'er me softly roll.

A tender joy that's only known to seem,
Came with that lovely childhood name, Lorene.

Ah! would you know the spell that bound the
    dream,
The name's my guardian angel Love, Lorene.

I'll glide on down my life's imbittered stream,
And list to angel songs from sweet Lorene.

VIVIAN.

Vivian! 'tis the music of my dreaming,
    The name that fills my heart with love;
Word that's sweeter than the bliss of seeming,
    A sample of the names above,
Lovely poem of an untold sweetness,
    A song that echoes through my soul,
Name that makes my cares take lightning fleet-
    ness,
    While blissful joys around me roll.

Vivian! name that wakes my longing,
  And bids me soar on tireless wing
Far above the atmosphere of wronging
  To honor's cool, refreshing spring;
Name that lifts my soul to fancies golden,
  Around the Eden home of love,
Bringing sweeter peace than known of olden,
  When Heaven sent its angel dove.

Vivian! name that makes me think of Aidenn,
  Sweet home that Future holds for me
And the fair and lovely angel maiden,
  Who'll bless my heart, and days to be.
Name that sings of sweeter hope and glory
  Than ever thrilled my heart of old,
And the one that prompts the old, old story
  Of love for her the name doth hold.

———————

MY MOTHER'S PRAYERS.

This vexing world of troubling cares
Has nothing sweet as mother's prayers;
They drive my trials far away,
And seem my only help and stay.

This sinful world of luring snares,
Has nothing good as mother's prayers;
They bear my thoughts to Heaven's home,
And keep my feet from vice to roam.

Oh! saintly mother's tender prayer!
'Tis richest blessing life can share.
O mother, pray! Thy prayers alone
Can for thy son's wrong deeds atone!

DOES MY DARLING PRAY FOR ME?

When the shades of evening gather,
   Borne on dusky wings of Night,
And fair Luna, through her pity,
   Comes to calm with soothing light;
When these hours of mellow moonlight,
   Smoothly glide o'er work and thee,
Till sweet sleep has called for Alice,
   Does my darling pray for me?

If a prayer of gentle whispers
   Fly to Heaven's throne for me,
From her soul so pure and holy,
   Then far stronger I would be.
All the strength of manhood's valor,
   All the courage left the free,
I would use for right and honor,
   If my darling prayed for me.

Ever since our first sweet meeting,
   While my heart has learned to love,
I have bowed before my dreaming,
   Asking angels from above
Then to hover round sweet Alice,
   Till the ghostly shades would flee,—
Praying love to make me holy—
   Did my darling pray for me?

MY LOVE.

I love to tell my love so well,
Because l love far more than well;
It can't be told, the love I hold,
From now until I'm gray and old.

I love with might and know it right
To love and feel love's fond delight.
I love the ease to bow my knees
And tell my love when no one sees.

I love to feel what hearts conceal,
For love is earth's sole joy and weal.
I love the bliss of love like this,
For no true love is found amiss.

I love with pride, and cannot hide
The love that will fore'er abide.
My love will live and always give
A charm to glad the years I live.

———————

The man with no preconceived harbor of purpose is as useless to the needy millions of humanity, as an aimless ship in mid-ocean, with sail spread, subject to be driven to and fro by changeable winds until wrecked on some unknown rocks. Load your vessel with the merchandisable exports from the peculiar products of your own individuality, hoist the flag of honor, and sail for a definite port of entry to the needs of humanity.

5

IN AN ALBUM.

May fragrant roses of the mind,
  Within you, find their native soil;
May grace and gentleness be twined
  Around you in a maiden foil.
May each recurring, blooming year,
  A virtue lend to rich your heart;
May every day, with duty done,
  Declare you did a noble part.

ALABAMA.

I am waiting, only waiting,
  Till this heavy year is o'er,
Then I'm bound for Alabama—
  For the Heaven she holds in store.
Ah! to meet my friends and loved ones,'
  Whom I left so long ago,
Would renew a golden pleasure
  Which the angels hardly know.

I am waiting, sadly waiting,
  For the greetings fond and true
In my own dear Alabama
  From the friends I always knew.
Parting gilds the chains of friendship
  With a gold undimmed by Time,
And my soul's inborn sincerity
  Makes the tie a bond divine.

I am longing, sweetly longing,
  For the gladsome, happy spring,
When to fond, dear Alabama,
  My glad heart will take its wing.
Spring! the emblem of my feelings,
  When that gracious time shall come—
When I'm happy and contented
  In my Alabama home.

I am waiting, gladly waiting,
  Till from work and cares I'm free,
When the smiles of Alabama
  Give the joy that's life to me.
No proud clime is kissed by Heaven,
  Like my fair, sweet native land:
Were I hunting earth's best garden,
  I would find thy winsome strand.

There the flowers bloom serenely
  In pure Nature's home retreat;
There sweet birds are joyous singing,
  Weary feelings to defeat;
There each streamlet echoes, faintly,
  Wooings of the god of Love;—
There a maiden land reposes,
  Fairest 'neath the stars above!

I am dreaming (happy dreaming!)
  Of this haven of my heart;
Thoughts of queenly Alabama,
  Never from my dreams depart.

I am far from her, but love her
  With a constancy unknown,
And think of her so proudly,
  Thoughts of other lands have flown.

When the shades of evening hover
  O'er thee, pious mother-land,
When thou kneelst in humble pleading
  For the guidance of God's hand,
Pray, invoke His gracious blessings
  On thy wayward, wandering boy,
Till again within thy bosom,
  He is safe from all annoy.

THE FATEFUL QUESTIONS.

Will you marry me and love me
  With a constancy unknown;
Will you live with me and bless me ·
  With the thought that you're my own?

Will you sow within my bosom,
  Seeds of gentleness and love;
Will you plant within my nature,
  Nine sweet virtues from above?

Will you glad our home's fair garden
  With the roses of the heart,
Will you stud the skies above it
  With the stars bright minds impart?

Will you cheer my life and soothe it
  With the sympathy of love,
Close it with a benediction,
  Fit to welcome it above?

ONLY LULA.

Only Lula is my darling,
  Whom 'tis Heav'n to linger near;
Only hours are fond and fleeting,
  When I'm calling her my dear!

Only words from her bring music,
  Echoing long within my soul;
Only eyes like hers are gentle
  With the azure they unroll.

Only forms like hers are graceful—
  Eloquent with winning charms;
Only she disturbs discretion,
  As love's magnet for my arms.

Only hair like hers is lovely,
  Luxuriant with dreamy curls;
Only hands like hers are fashioned
  For the fairest, sweetest girls.

Only lips like hers are tempting,
  Luscious with an apple hue;
Only honeyed fees of parting,
  Are the joys for which I sue.

Only Lula is my darling,
  Whom I love with all love's might!
Only Lula has attractions,
  Drawing me to her each night.

ONLY WAITING.

I am waiting, only waiting,
  Till the twilight hours appear,
When I'm happy as an angel
  With my darling Lula near;
Then the fleeting hourlets whisper
  Of fair future's siren charm—
Of the soothing draughts of pleasure
  When our life is arm in arm.

I am waiting (anxious waiting!)
  Till the stillness of the night
Thrills my soul, to take me quickly
  To my heart's enrobed delight.
Far more vied than kingly favor,
  Is love's welcome in her eye;
Blessing me so much, I envy
  Not a man below the sky.

I am waiting (fondly waiting!
  Till the evening vespers chime,
Then, the thrills of love reneweth
  With her lily hand in mine.

Ah! the joys that linger round me,
  Wafting bliss so very near,
While my eyes drink in her sweetness
  And my lips pronounce her dear!

I am waiting, I am longing
  For her promise to be true—
For the cheer of union-music
  Till my life and hers are through;
For the balm of love to soothe me
  With the gentleness of peace,
For my love and hers to bless me,
  Till my life and hers shall cease.

My heart is echoing responses to your oft-repeated promise of a Heaven-honored, blissful time, when the melancholy strains of longing and the plaintive tunes of hope will cease to be marred by the discords of uncertainty, and will join in a lovely harmony with the enchanting songs of conjugal love, soothing music of the heart's realization, and the enlivening anthem refrains of happiness; when Joy and Peace will never grow weary dancing to the music, and Content will ever be entranced in admiration; when all will blend into a glory-tuned song to enrapture, continually, our envied home in Fruition, until life's music shall cease and her harps be unstrung.

STANDING AT THE DOOR.

Fond bliss enstores a dainty treat,
　　Standing at the door;
The kings ne'er had such joy complete,
　　In the days of yore.

'Twould take the help of ages old,
　　With their endless lore,
To tell the love that's often told,
　　Standing at the door!

But few have learned the magic power
　　When the day is o'er,
To put life's sweets in one short hour,
　　Standing at the door.

When clasped hands are feeling thrills,
　　Longed for evermore,
The heart-throbs tell what ecstasy wills,
　　Standing at the door.

There's other happenings sweeter far!
　　But can't tell you more,
For fear 'twill all my bliss debar,
　　Standing at the door.

DO YOU LOVE ME?

Do you love me darling, tell me,
  Does your heart respond to mine?
For I love you, darling, fondly,
  With that feeling called divine!

Do you love me, darling, tell me?
  Let me feel life's only bliss;
For I love you, darling, only,
  And your love I cannot miss.

Though I feel it, let me know it,
  Let your words bring ceaseless joy;
Let them fall, like Heavenly manna,
  To give life where doubts destroy.

Though your eyes flash welcome gleamings,
  From their sparkling depths of blue;
Though I feel it, nearly know it,
  That you love me fondly, too,

Still I crave the sweet assurance
  And the music of the words,
Which alone can make me happy
  With the gushing joy of birds!

SOUTH CAROLINA.

Carolina! Carolina!
There's a glory in thy name;
From thy wisdom and thy valor
Thou hast won a deathless fame.
Dauntless heroes awed the British,
In those history-making years,
When young Freedom's banner floated
In a gloom of doubt and fears.

Honor to thy peerless Marion,
Sumter, Pickens, and thy Lee,
Who from dread despair won victory,
Gaining liberty for thee;
Laurels for thy humble Jasper,
Who reset thy flag to wave
With a pride of daring courage
O'er the noblest of the brave!

Praises to the timely efforts
Of thy "City by the Sea,"
To give succor to our army
While it fought to make us free;
'Twas when Northern ports had fallen
Prey to England's might and greed,
And the valiant North States trembled
When our army came to need.

Great and many were thy statesmen
After Freedom came to stay,
And the mantles of their greatness
Have been worn till our own day.
Great Calhoun still towers grandly
In the trio of our pride;
Robert Hayne, the South's debater,
Won allegiance to our side.

History culls from South Carolina
Priceless legacies (so rare),
Of unparalleled devotion
By her daughters, brave as fair;
Emily—embodiment of valor—
In a maiden's queenly grace,
Won from loyal hearts the tribute:
"Bravest, sweetest of our race!"

And fair Dicey, for her frequent daring,
Shared the glory of applause;
Mrs. Dillard saved an army—
Angel to young Freedom's cause!
And true patriotism renders
Mrs. Mott a cherished fame;
Hundreds more deserve a mention,
As the builders of a name.

Mexico will speak in praises,
Such as conquered tongues proclaim,
Of Palmetto's vict'rious regiment,
Which has been consigned to fame.

In our recent bloody struggle
South Carolina was the first
To secede, and first the thunder
Of the war upon her burst.

Still, as years roll in the future,
  Noble sons and daughters rise,
Worthy of our favored country—
  Fairest 'neath the bending skies.
Emulate your sires, conspicuous
  For their virtues and their might;
Gild your names on deeds illustrious,
  For your Southland and for right.

————————

Back in the dear dead years of Southern glory,
when the balmy breezes of our fragrant Southland bore to a friendly world the sweet aroma of
virtuous lives and deeds, which bloomed in perennial spring-exuberance beneath our favoring skies,
Heaven, so proud of our garden land, gave to her
Henry Timrod, a sweet singer, with a gentle voice
of pathos and tenderness, to sing of her beauty
and glory, to trace the matchless symmetry of her
bending skies, and to pipe eulogiums of praise to
her noble sons and fair daughters.

FALSE.

False! the sobbing winds bemoan it.
  As the grief of all my years;
Whispering breezes long have borne it,
  Like a prescience born of fear.

False! the constant stars are twinkling,
  Stars, they only heard our plight.
Feverish tears, the thought is sprinkling
  O'er dead love's forsaken night.

False! no thought was fond or fragrant,
  Till it bowed beneath the throne
Sacred to those eyes so radiant,
  There to worship thee alone.

False! no work was sweet or pleasant,
  But that done to give thee joy;
Love made me an humble peasant,—
  Happy as thy errand boy.

False! no dreams had peace without thee
  Queen of every phantom part—
'Twas mirage so turned about thee
  From thy image in my heart.

Go, false joy and hope, forever,
  Still I'll never bow to thee,
Though 'twould turn the tides that sever;
  To God alone, I bend my knee.

I have manhood still unshaken
   And a courage born of pride
Which can ne'er be overtaken
   By the eyes and lips that lied.

I am glad 'twas you proved faithless
   To the feeling oft exprest;
For if I had proven faithless,
   'Twould have robbed my life of rest.

To betray a queenly maiden
   In the trust of constant love,
To forsake a heart enladen
   With the virtues from above.

To prove false to worded passion,
   Caught from flames that burn the heart,—
Chill Remorse would lose compassion;
   Conscience thrust its piercing dart.

So farewell, and if forever,
   May the will of Fate prove best.
And perchance the years that sever
   May bring each a love more blest.

NATURE'S MODEL POEM.

Nature has one model poem
  Wrote to woo the poet's heart—
Wrote to wean him from the faulty,
  Soulless verse of studied art.

Twenty years of gushing springtime,
  Nature's buddings of the mind
Were implanted in this poem
  To enrich it o'er its kind.

Twenty summers filled with sweetness,
  Nature sipped life's nectar—love,
For the passion of this poem,
  Thrilled by touch of Muses' glove.

Twenty autumns, tinged with saffron,
  Nature harvested the gold
Of rich thought and deep emotion,
  For this poem of his mould.

Twenty winters, angel feathers
  Fell to whiten earth impure;
Nature gathered all their virtues,
  That his poem would be pure.

Twenty years of fairy beauty,
  Nature chose a grace unseen
For a measure and a rhythm,
  Faultless as a flowing stream.

Now the work of years is finished,
   Built upon a breath divine—
Masterpiece of Nature's genius,
   Graced with music and with rhyme.

And the title of this poem
   Shows an Idyl from above;
'Tis the spirit of the poem
   Felt by all, as "MADE TO LOVE."

Nature, modest as a maiden,
   Rich in worth, unwooed by fame,
Hides this charming master-poem
   From immortelles of name.

Only friends and cherished loved ones
   Read his work of hidden art:
And I, favored of the favored,
   Will it all my pride and heart.

This sweet poem is a maiden
   Whom a Raphael might defy
To portray the hidden beauty
   Of her soul and gentle eye.

And the poets and the painters
   Of the present and the past,
Ne'er have had a queenlier model
   To inspire a perfect task.

She has given my soul its music,
  And my thoughts their gentle rhyme;
She has made my heart a poet,
  With emotions all sublime!

And I'll sing of her, the Lovely,
  Till the coming years shall pine
For one look at her rare beauty —
  This fair maiden-Love of mine.

And the world of song shall know her,
  Through the tribute of my rhyme,
As the fairest sweetest maiden
  Who has trod the shores of Time.

ALABAMA.

Though thy present's brown and sear,
Silvery dawnings linger near;
For thy fame is everyrwhere,
                    Alabama.

Westward empires wind their way,
Following sunset's golden ray—
Now has come thy bridal day,
                    Alabama.

Thou art past thy trying days,
Dark with shameful mist and haze,
And a future charms thy gaze,
                    Alabama.

Springtime comes with budding trees,
Fragrance floats on every breeze—
Progress brings thee days like these,
Alabama.

There is treasure in thy hills,
Money in thy coming mills,
Lavished wealth fond Heaven wills
Alabama.

Harvests rich bring forth rare spoil
From the pleasant faithful toil
On thy varied, fertile soil,
Alabama.

There's a murmur in thy streams,
Sweet as music in our dreams,
And love's paradise it seems—
Alabama.

Flowers glad thy dreamy dells,
Still a sweeter beauty dwells
In thy bonnie, blooming belles,
Alabama.

And thy sons by merit rise,
To the sphere where honor lies;
There they pride thy doting eyes,
Alabama.

Tis Elysium of the West,
Said by Greeks, the land most blest,
Where the mighty heroes rest,
                    Alabama.

If a land be Heaven's pride,
Where its beauties e'er abide—
'Tis our State—'tis not denied,
                    Alabama.

SICKENING WHEN YOU'RE NOT "IN IT."

Did you ever see two lovers
  Strolling through the soft moonlight,
When they had the sweet assurance
  That no others were in sight?—

Hand in hand, they whisper softly
  More than Cupid ever heard;
Then they squeeze each hand the tighter
  After every loving word.

On they walk with tortoise slowness,
  Feeling thrilled with earthly bliss;
And monotony, to vary,
  Oft they stop, caress, and kiss.

He forgets and leaves around her
  His left arm, though on they go,
Caring not to lose such pleasure,
  As the neighbors will not know.

Fear intrudes his cruel presence—
  Every sound disturbs her wits,
Forcing way his arm so quickly
  From the waist it warmly fits.

Every eve they wish it over,
  Just as hitherto defined;
"Cuss" they will, but can't express it,
  When a couple's close behind.

TO S. F. M.

You wear a sunny, blushing smile,
Shown through a merry laughing wile,
That wakes the feelings of my heart
And longing thoughts of love impart.

Your large, soft, tender, radiant eyes
Are beaming through my wistful sighs:
They hold a depth of azure blue—
A fairy heaven, for some man's due!

Your wavy wealth of flaxen hair
Enshrines a charming beauty rare;
Your sandy, silken, circling curls
Enthrone you queen of lovely girls.

Your full, soft, pearly, glowing face
Is fashioned with a nameless grace;
Your form is all the Grecian mould,
Improved upon the type of old.

My tribute will not be complete,
Unless I falter at your feet,
And to your modest ears make known
The height to which my love has grown.

I offer you a faithful heart—
It's wounded now by Cupid's dart.
I'll vow my love forever true,
If constancy remain in you.

But you're so gentle, fair, and sweet,
To be your mate I feel unmeet;
But if my heart you don't refuse,
I'll give you love and honor's dues.

THE FLIRT'S POLICY.

I'll vum! the luck is 'dogged' bad—
  A score of sweethearts Christmas times;
I'll own I look a 'kinder' sad
  To think how they will take the dimes.

I've tried to fuss and break the "case"
  With every one of them you see;
But each one holds me to the race,
  And says "you can't lose me, Charlie."

They call me sweet and "hoo doo" names
When present giving times are near,—
They know the cards in all the games,
And throw my "pockets out of gear."

VIVIAN'S EYES.

There are glories that gleam like an angel's dream,
From the radiant sunset skies;
There are splendors that stream from the morning
beam,
When the bride of the day doth rise;
But they in their pride have never defied
The beauty of Vivian's eyes.

The lustrous stars, with their golden bars—
The diamond gems of the skies,
Whose sparkles so bright enrapture the night
With a glory that nevermore dies,
Are scarcely as bright as the radiant light
That twinkles in Vivian's eyes.

The lily of the vale has a sweet little tale,
That the nymphs and the fairies prize;—
An angel willed that her smile be instilled,
And now in the lily it lies;
But the sweet lily fair can never compare
With the sweetness of Vivian's eyes.

The tenderness shown in the Southern dome,—
 In the mild, sweet summerland skies,
Like the smiles of love from the Saviour above,
 Are as gentle as a maiden's sighs;
But their tenderest place has never a trace
Of the tenderness of Vivian's eyes.

They are windows divine to Virtue's shrine—
 The purest below the skies;
More tender and true than the ages knew
 In their queens of the heart and its ties;—
So pardon my sighs and frequent cries
For a gaze at Vivian's eyes.

PARTING THROBS.

The night bewails the sadness
 That we must part;
The morning brings no gladness
 To cheer our heart!

The winds are softly blowing
 Their sad refrain,
But none on earth are knowing
 Our cureless pain!

The starlets twinkle sadly
 Their pity-cry;
My heart beats—oh! so madly—
 To say good-bye!

You'll wait in vain my coming,
  Each silent eve;
And with the night wind's humming,
  You'll sit and grieve !

And while love songs you're singing—
  Those songs we sang,
From every word, upspringing,
  Will dart a pang !

Dear Love, we know the anguish
  Of burning tears;
And oh! we'll have to languish
  For gloomy years !

Our eyes will tell the story,
  In accents sad,
Of love's departed glory
  And Heaven we had!

The bloom of life will wither,—
  The bloom joys give,
And oft we'll wonder whether
  'Tis best to live.

O God of Love and Heaven!
  Is there no balm
That parted souls are given
  To bring life's calm?

THE OLD REVELATION.

I love a maiden; if twill please
Your heart, I'll say "I love Louise."
If not, I'll heave a wistful sigh
And, longing, glance at your soft eye,
Then look toward Heaven, and sadly pray
To meet a loved one some sweet day.

Yet if your heart and eyes respond
To all my feelings warm and fond,
Like tendrils of the leaning vine,
My love would round you firmly twine;
And in its fond and gentle grace
Would live and die, in your embrace.

LET ME TRY.

Ambition bids my soul arise
And soar to heights beyond these skies;
A hell 'twould be, to crawl and die
Upon the earth! oh, let me try!

And Duty makes me e'er believe
Tis noble only to achieve.
Attempting brings a blessing nigh
To soothe the hearts of those who try.

And if a storm dissolve in air
Our every prospect, sweet and fair,
There's peace that fate cannot deny
To bless the unknown souls who try.

If others soar the topmost height,
And we've not wings for lofty flight;
Let's *climb* the summit ere we die
And learn God blesses those who try.

If work refund no ample store—
A happy conscience wills us more,
And Heaven gives what earth denies,
For God rewards each one who tries!

If marble shaft do not proclaim:—
"HE LIVES IMMORTAL HERE WITH FAME."
This worthy tribute's not denied
To any humble soul:—"HE TRIED!"

EVENING'S FOND RETREAT.

When the evening brings the shadows
    With a quietness to calm;
Day just fled with all its labor,
    Love suggests a soothing balm—
How to spend the wintry evening
    Pleasantly as kings would please,
Only down the street to wander
    To the home of sweet Louise.

There the hours in fleetness vanish,
  Breathing o'er me fond delight,
While I gaze upon her sweetness—
  Charmed to stay within her sight.
Ah! such moments are so happy,
  Cheering me with peaceful ease;
Thankful for the precious blessing,
  Just to see and love Louise.

Oft I plead with her to love me
  As a sweetheart fond and true;
But a "no" rewards my pleading
  With a chill and heartache too.
Still she asks me "not to leave her,
  Looking for another, please;"
And to show her all my kindness,
  I remain with sweet Louise.

Yet I'd go and cease to love her,
  Leaving with a wistful sigh,
But I plainly can discover
  Hope—a kindness in her eye,
And a welcome in her features;
  So again, when no one sees,
I renew my earnest pleading
  For the love of sweet Louise.

Blessed are the hours of twilight,
  Happy are the hearts they blend;
Joyous are the hours of wooing,
  Sweet the blissful peace they send.

Ever welcome hour of evening,
Soothing is thy quiet breeze;
Then I'm happy and contented
With my bonnie, sweet Louise.

. ———————

SONNET.

The pilgrim, fleeing from the land of sin,
When worn with travel, sick of burning sun,
Kneels gladly in the calm when day is done,
   And lifts his eyes, in prayer, to Heaven's glen
   Where twinkle stars of hope and peace for him;
Just so, I haste from out the cheerless throng,
Who have no love to sweetly glad life's song,
   And loathing care's annoying weary din
   I bow in twilight's calm before your feet;
And look with prayer into those answering skies
Which lie empearled within your sparkling eyes,
Where thoughts of love, like twinkling starlets,
   shine,
And promise "Heaven to me when you are mine;"
Come soothe my life, fond Love's long sought
   retreat!

PART II.

A LIVING HEROINE.

DEDICATED TO THE W. C. T. U. AND I. O. G. T.

I.

I have a sad tale that fain I'd tell:
'Tis fraught with a wish that long t'will well
   Encourage the vows that conquer crime.
In years that have gone I used to meet
A maiden of youth's fond smiles and sweet,
   Though passed she the years of youthful prime.

Oh, bright were her eyes with virtue's grace!
And beauty had kissed her rosy face,
   Then quietly losing it's glow;
How could it e'er fade from nature's shrine,
Ah, would it e'er be embalmed as mine!
   Was ever my prayer to know.

The light of Christ's love had blest her days,
Which charmed me so with her winning ways;
   House cares she would never shirk;
A thrifty wife is a husband's pride,
Her happy smiles on every side,
   Are mirrored in her work.

So lovely and sweet the songs we sang,
In unison our voices then rang
  The music of God and love.
Such charms had those songs for her and me,
It seemed that our hearts would melted be,
  To join, like the souls above.

My heart then gave life to words of love,
Expecting such back like coos of dove.
  Alas! I heard no reply.
It seemed that she liked me more than all,
And always looked pleased when I would call—
  But could not she love me, why?

A mystery's there that caused me woe;
I prayed her to tell. I longed to know
  Just why she couldn't love me then.
In secret she told her story sad,
While down o'er her cheeks flowed tears as mad
  With sighs that "It might have been."

II.

"It's not the old tale of love untrue;
For he was the truest one I knew,
  Or ever expect to know.
Oh! John was so gentle, mild, and kind—
So lovely was he, in heart and mind,
  My love toward him did grow.

"Quite often he came to bring a smile,
Which caused one returned, from me, the while
   Though short, that he spent with me;
For surely it seemed, mad time would fly,
Then ever so rashly, swiftly by,
   That ten came at eight, to be.

"The days and the months stole fast away;
My heart with its love grew bright as May
   When woods are so green with life.
Oh! that I could see more days as bright—
Oh! that I could dream more dreams at night
   So free, *like* those days, from strife.

"Full many a day of azure blue,
We sailed on the river, just us two;
   So smooth were the flow and glide,
It seemed that the coming days would flow
As calm through the years of life below,
   If he would e'er be my guide.

"Just like the mild flow of the waters one,
Our hearts seemed to join, to run
   In unison evermore.
True hearts which are bound by nature's will,
Will meet like the rills from sides of hill,
   No matter what might ignore.

"My cup for lifetime seemed blest with love.
Ah! sweet were its sips like those above—
The drink of the angels bright.
This life would a desert be, and cold,
Without in each heart, true love, to hold
Poor way-faring man a light.

"He said I was e'er his guiding star,
And hope's fairest prize, then near or far,
Which long he had wished to gain.
He said that his days were bright and fair,
While trying to win a heart so rare,
Like snow, which is free from stain.

"And just then he said 'will you be mine,
And take me, dear one, to e'er be thine,
As long as our hearts shall live?
Oh! be my loved rose to sweeten my life,
Enticing me home from sin and strife,
To bask in the smiles you give.'

" 'How could you say more, my dear, my own!
This moment has made my heart full grown,
Embalmed in a cup of bliss!
Of course, dearest John, our souls are one,
Ordained to be so when God begun
To form a sweet world like this!'

III.

"Remembered, that hour and always will,
That witnessed these words for Fate to kill
  Their hopes; for it soon did rend
Sweet music, from heart both tuned to play
The songs of true love, mid smiles of May.
  Alas! for those songs again.

"At night, when I knelt in secret prayer,
Quite often I longed to ask God spare
  My John from all trials sore.
Oh, sad! but I never asked Him to—
Unnumbered the woes it's brought me through,
  Repenting it evermore!

"I thought he would shun the Tempter's snare—
Ah! sin could ne'er stain a soul so rare,
  Nor ruin a *true* heart so pure!
But frost ever seeks the sweetest flowers,
And woodmen e'er hunt the fairest bowers—
  How can earthly bloom endure?

"The evil Seducer set a snare,
On which he had hoped to mildly bear
  My John to that place of doom.
The flowers that bud most tender here,
Are culled by his hand, which plucks them where
  They smile, with their sweetest bloom.

7

"You see we had built a castle grand.
Alas! for its base was earthly sand,
  Which crumbles, and *madly* falls
Headlong into Misery's ocean doom,
And drowns Expectation's hopeful bloom;
  Ne'er to deck more castle walls!

IV.

"The hours seemed to hunt that sweet May day,
The birds were to sing our wedding lay—
  Uniting our lives for time.
Then Happiness, flower of earth's fair dell,
Was growing in loveliness, to tell,
  Our hearts would make perfect rhyme.

"The night just before our wedding day,
Midnight's lonely tongue had held its sway,
  Before I could find sweet sleep.
Then dreamed I saw buried a drunken soul,
But Virtue and name he'd buried in bowl
  And covered with years so deep!

"Another—once fair—now thin and pale!
What bruised, care-worn face, tear-furrowed,
  frail! —
  Great scars on her face and arm!
Her eyes! what a book of woes reveal!
Dead hopes had their graves where looks conceal
  Not much of their faded charm.

"This mother, his wife, alone could cry,
From others no tears, not yet a sigh
   For rum-ruined man so vile.
Small children in rags there cried for bread;
But one, nearly grown, by father led,
   Was drunk as a fool the while.

"One bright little girl, in accents sweet,
Then said: 'Oh, don't cry, mamma. Pa beat
   You so every time he drinks!
He's mean; let him die and go away
Where whisky men go and have to stay.
   He never loved us, I thinks.'

"But still the grieved mother sobbed and mourned.
She thought of the trials, troubles borne!
   Her son, now her only stay,
Was wrecked by his sire, who sealed a doom
Upon the young boy, just in life's bloom;
   For plucked is the bud to-day!

"I saw the sad wife and mother leave
The drunkard's lone grave. Who could but grieve!
   A sermon of truth and woe
Was preached in the tread of shoeless feet,
That went to a home that once was neat—
   Now owned by rumseller, though!"

V.

"I woke and my eyes were wet with tears.
What could all this mean, my dream and fears?
  My wondering ceased in sleep.
Another dread vision filled with fear!
A gallows and hundreds standing near,
  All eyes were about to weep.

"My God! the same mother as before,
And children round her, an bleeding sore,
  Their hearts were still full of woe!
A sheriff then led a boy, eighteen,
Around to the scaffold,—horrid scene!
  Alas! 'twas the boy I know,

"Who went to his father's grave so drunk.
He stood in the face of death, but shrunk
  At first, as he saw his fate.
Then said he in lone and dread despair:
'I have but a farewell breath to share,
  And Hope it will be too late.

" ' 'Tis rum that has brought me here to die;
Next moment will be my last cold sigh.
  I'll go like a flash to hell
And meet my doomed father who gave me
The first cursed drink! Oh! friends you see
  That rum will our souls soon sell!'

"So ended his fate. His mother wild,
Was carried to the poorhouse. Every child
  Was bound to some friends for life.
The mother heart-broken, sad and lone,
Soon died of her grief, with none to moan
  Her death, as she passed from strife.

"Her face was quite like some old true friend,
Just so the drunken man's, but thoughts would
    tend
  Back to the young boy just hung.
What crime had he done to bring such doom?
I asked one to tell what plucked the bloom
  That from life's sweet stem was wrung?

"He said that the boy had won a heart—
A good, fair young girl promised to part
  From under paternal care.
Her father and mother wouldn't consent.
The boy, in a rage, when drunk, then rent
  Life's chords, from her parents rare!"

VI.

This horrible sin and crime so great—
The strain of excitement made her wake
  To a fearful silent gloom!
"This awful sad dream! what can it be?
O Fate! is it life's gall cup for me?
  Must I bear an earthly doom?"

O'er her cheeks, rolled glad and saddening tears,
In her mind rose hopes accompanied with fears;
 Soon a light began to steal
Through the room; she thought it hailed anxious
  Day,
So she opened a door for Morning's glad ray,
 Her dread loneliness to heal.

But Egyptian darkness of gloomy, weird night,
Was the greeting received by her awe-stricken
  sight!
 Fiery fiends and wild ghosts filled the air!
Lo! among them she saw drunken crews of
  gambling men.
Some were young, but all darkened with vice
  and with sin,
 But the sight was too horrid to bear!

So trembling, ghostly pale, quickly bolted she
  the door,
With a painful lone feeling that never before
 Had thrilled her with such vague unknown woe.
Then suddenly she thought of the mystical light,
That had kept the whole room still so won-
  drously bright,
 And the thoughts made her restlessness go.

Not knowing what to do, to send thoughts far
  away,
She began then to play a new temperance lay.
 And so feelingly, softly to sing.

She was thinking of times when her lover was
    there,
When she'd sung the same song—not noting the
    wild glare
Of his eyes, while the music would ring:—

SONG.

If ever you are straying
    Around a saloon;
You needn't come praying
    To walk with me soon.

CHORUS.

The man that drinks liquor,
    Will never be mine;
The wife of such tricker,
    Will sadly repine.

If ever you're gambling
    Or playing at night,
You'll never be rambling
    With me in moonlight.

If ever you're cursing
    Where people can hear,
You'll never be nursing
    Your pet "little dear."

Go on with your drinking,
  And revel in wine;
But still you're not thinking
  You'll ever be mine.

Oh! yes, you will leave it,
  And quickly reform;
But the woman will grieve it
  Who enters the storm.

So you needn't be drinking,
  Nor duding it through,
If ever you're thinking
  My heart you will woo.

It was sung in sincerity and truth's feeling tone,
And determination of the strongest she'd known,
  Made her kneel for a sacred life vow:
"I will never, O God, place my life on hell's
    brinks,
Just to marry a man who continually drinks—
  'Tis my honor's own pledge to Thee now!"

Her blue eyes were sparkling, and the light re-
    mained,
While a silent, sweet stillness over all things
    reigned,
  With a charm like the sirens have won;
Then a voice far sweeter than earth's mortals
    had known,
And a lily-white hand was caressing her own,
  As an angel maid said "Oh, well done;

"I have come to warn you, sweet maiden, good
and true,
This sad vision you've seen is the future for you,
If you marry the one whom you love;
For he drinks, and your joys he will ever ensnare,
Be not grieved, for hereafter you'll bloom over
there,
In the home of the happy Above."

What would we do were it not for angels bright—
Some guardian loved one from the blue,
To warn us all of foes that come at night—
The dangers which we never knew.
Oh, blessed thought! fair ministering angel bands
Will leave their glory-home to guard these lands
Till darkest trials are through!

Before those sad, heart-rending words were said
Pale Lillie fell back on the floor.
The light went out and darkness came instead—
A gloom for many days in store,
Came o'er her when the angel left her sight.
She moaned and wrung her hands and cried out-
right,
"O God! Oh, let me live no more!

"Oh, take me home! my guardian angel, fair!
Oh, bliss! if I could only die!
My God! this cup is more than I can bear!
O John! my John! why do I cry?

Ten thousand curses on the demon drink!
I'd shoot the wretch who led to ruin's brink
  My noble John! Sweet death come nigh!

"My dream! a drunkard's wife! what woes await
A miserable, mean drunkard's cursed wife!
My vow!—I'll never be a drunkard's mate!
  Lord, no! I'll live a lonely life,
Without my John—without a hope instead,
And lose my love, my joy, and beg for bread,
  Before I'll bear a drunkard's strife!

"My happy days of love and peaceful joy—
  They're gone! they're dead! to live no more!
And I, sad fate! am bound to grief's annoy—
  No peace can future hold in store.
Sad woman's fate! thus chained to face her
  doom,
While man may roam the world to find its bloom,
  And shun the scene of living gore.

"O woman! curse this hell-made liquor, vile;
  For since the fall of mother Eve,
The bowl has nursed the serpent's tempting guile,
  Our doting loved ones to deceive.
I hate! despise! abhor! this Satan snare,
That kills the peace which comes to woman's
  share,
And makes her live to mourn and grieve!

"O woman! come, let's arm ourselves to fight
 This heartless foe that dooms our way.
Maybe, some gallant men will lend their might,
 And make their votes and speeches sway.
Our fall will fill the land with ceaseless woe;
Our gain will bring prosperity's o'erflow.
 Let's work and fight and hope and pray."

Her anguished heart, with ghostly fears o'ercast,
 Of scarry, frightful, ugly mein,
Then brought a lulling spell of fainting fast.
 A fever soon disturbed her brain.
Sweet fancy, still submissive to desire,
Soon fills her mind with quiet love-lit fire—
 She lives some happy hours again.

The evening rays are smiling through their gold,
 The cloudless sky is azure still,
The lovely flowers. sweet petals unfold,
 The waters murmur in the rill,
The birds playing, chirping, sweet and low,
And breezes gently from the westward blow,
 As they walk slowly down the hill.

Her John puts cedar twigs around her hair,
 Among her nightly raven curls,
"I live for you—'tis all I ask to share
 Your life, oh loveliest one of girls."
She plucks the ivy white and crimson red,
To shade his heart when he so sweetly said:
 "You are most precious of the pearls."

They've wandered to the clear, cool river now,
  And watch the many fishes swim.
The weeping willow bends her drooping bow
  Around the lovers graced and true.
Their hearts, too full to speak, their lips now
    meet,
In kisses loving, fond, and heavenly sweet,—
  So fond, a queen would envy them!

Soon the tender full voice of Lillie rose in song,
  So sweet, angels would listen to hear.
Her lover imagined 'twas a siren love-throng
  That were singing to charm him more near:

SONG.

Will the bright glowing rays of the morning
  Fill our souls with the heart's wedding lay?
Will Hymen's bridal sweetness be adorning
  All our days with the beauty of May?

CHORUS.

Where the roses of love, sweetly tender,
  Are budding to bloom angel-fair,
And the joy-bells of song ever render
  A bliss, for our hearts' happy share.

Will the downy, soft wings of Favor,
  E'er hover o'er the paths that we roam?
Will the blessings of our dear Savior,
  Be showered in the future's sweet home?

In the solemn, delightful silence, a clear tone,
Sweetly filled with its echo, her heart's torrid
   zone—
'Twas a song from her lover so dear :—

SONG.

We will live in the happy, fond Aidenn,
  In a home, which your smiles will adorn;
And the music of love will be laden
With the life cheering rays of the morn.

CHORUS.

Let your head on my heart be lying,
  And your eyes looking kindly in mine;
While I kiss away tears, which are tenderly
   drying
On your cheeks, as you lovingly recline.

Yes, my Love, Lillie fair, sweet To-morrow,
  Will unite our true hearts evermore;
And the smiles of kind Fortune will borrow
All the joy that this life has in store.

If lovers' dreams had their fruition,
  Aspiring hopes, their peaceful Aidenn;
Our hearts would feel no deep contrition,
  Our homes would have no pining maiden.

If love could keep it's secret heaven,
   And lips could hold a loving kiss;
We'd need no future to be given,
   This earth would be a home of bliss.

And could our minds the mystic future scan,
   And see our troubles held in store,
We'd all give o'er and ne'er the courage man
   To climb the Alpine steep before.
If only could we in life's morn begin
Our journey with mistakes reversed again,
   We'd sail a calmer day to shore

The lovers still are sharing fancy's dream,—
A boat sails down the rapid flowing stream
   And lands close by the lovers' side,
The name of boat, WHISKY, bright letters gleam
"BOUND FOR DESTRUCTION—PLEASURE RIDE;"
A rough, strong wretch, with mocking, angry
      lip,
Then grasped her darling John, with firmest grip,
   And bore him off on rolling tide.

A shriek, more loud and wild than maiden tongue,
In all past woes, had ever thrilled the air and
      wrung
   The sleeping ears till all awoke,
Was heard, in rending tones, from Lillie's room,
Her parents and her sisters were there soon,
   To see what danger it bespoke.

Fair blooming Lillie, eldest one of eight,
To their surprise and trembling horror great,
   Was found there fainted on the floor! .
Their joys, their hopes, from Fancy's happy
     height,
Then fell, so lightning fast, to gloom of night!—
   In joy and grief we've equal store.

O world of change! O hopes and dreams of bliss!
O fallen peace! O troubling love like this!—
   So happy sweet and flowery fair,
That heaven it holds in every trusting heart—
Yet full of pain and woe, all share a part
   Of hell, in what they have to bear!

Were none of earth, though, found to be unkind—
Were all of pure and virtue-loving mind,
   Who deign to love in times like this—
Were whisky sent forever from our land,
We'd have young men, more noble, true and
     grand,
   And love would keep its secret bliss.

VII.

With all my skill, my pen cannot portray
The gloom and grief that hovered night and day,
   For long, sad weeks round Lillie's form,
As fever tossed her restless, aching brain;
Unconscious, though, of all her piercing pain,
   Her fancies reveled through the storm.

Would time were given, long, with which to tell
The dreams, some sad, some gay, that oft did
  dwell
Upon her mind, while in this trance—
Her frequent journeys to the river dark—
The river Death, where cried she to embark—
This all would make a long romance.

One warm day, while her fever was raging so
  hot and so high,
That her parents and all her acquaintances
  thought she would die,
In a trance, the last time, to Death's river, she
  went;
Many weary, lone hours, did she pace o'er the
  long trodden shore,
While she cried to pass o'er to the heav'n that
  her hopes had in store—
To the haven of bliss and its sweet enjoyment.

She was longing to cross from this world and
  its grief,
Far beyond all its troubles annoyed with care,
To the shore decked with flowers, affording
  relief
And a balm for the soul that had sorrow to
  share.

Still she gazed on the Spring laden land, blooming sweet,
  With a beauty unseen, and a grandeur unknown, ·
Happy angel-tuned songs, with a music complete,
  Lillie's ears then enticed from the balmy breeze
  blown,

From the shore of perennial Spring, laden sweet
  With the fragrance of flow'rs and the music ·
  of love.
Twas the borderland fair, of the heav'nly
  retreat;
  Far beyond was the home of our Savior above.
She was thrilled and entranced with the love-
  mirrored scene;
  So she rushed to the brink, but the boatman
  refused
To ferry her across to the tropical green.
  From a rapture, she fell with her heart sorely
  bruised,

And cried: "Boatman, oh! pilot me across
  To where my guardian angel lives!
Ah! leave me not lost love's heartrending cross,
  But bear me to the balm God gives
To those who suffer long life's paining sore.
  Ah! wilt thou leave me here alone
And haunt me with lost hope's sad *Nevermore*,
  And doom me still to live and moan?

8

"My mother taught me that when sore oppressed,
  When pain and anguish wrung my brow,—
When hope and life and love had left my breast,
  That God in mercy would allow
For me the gates of pearl to open wide
  And take me from my troubling grief,
To place me by my guardian angel's side,
  Where e'er I'd live in blest relief.

"O angel band! come bear me from this shore,
  Where false and luring fancy's dream
Brings hope and love and joy in blissful store,
  So full of sweets that only seem.
Oh! take me to that land where hope can live,
  Where love can hold its blissful joy:
Where happy dreams their own fruition give,
  And snares no more our loved decoy."

She turned to see the throng that crossed,
  She watched Death's boatman come and go;
Most all, into the darksome stream, he tossed,
  And they were washed to hell below;
But some were carried safely o'er the tide
  And landed on the Aidenn shore.
Their loved ones met them on that blissful side,
  And greeting angels sang before.

Forsaken Lillie saw the badge, "DUTY,"
  That shone upon the welcomed band,
In gleaming gold and radiant beauty:
  It was the passport to God's land.

The angels wore a badge of rainbow hue,
  Which on their forehead beamed; 'twas "Love,"
Resplendently, its golden beamings threw
  A radiance o'er the Home above.

Soon she beheld just over her own heart,
  The same gold badge of Love, so sweet,
"Ah, now!" she thought, "I'll make a safe
    embark
And with my angel maid, I'll meet,
Who came to warn me of my woes to bear—
  To show me horrid Fate to shun;
And said I'd bud and bloom forever there,
  Where laurel wreaths fair brows have won."

But no, the boatman still refused to take
  Her 'cross the surging billows dark;
But soon her angel came for mercy's sake
  To comfort Lillie's breaking heart.
Her Guardian Angel said, with greeting smile,
  Yet with a look that pity gave,
"Where is your badge of Duty, fair grieved child,
  To show that in Right's cause you're brave?"

"Dear Guardian Angel, see, I wear this: Love—
  I loved one with my heart and soul;
You wear this badge and so do all above;
  Don't this far more than Duty hold?"
"Ah, trusting maid! you loved but one, of all
  God's many children, loved and dear,
On whom, alike, His rays of mercy fall,
  And for whom Christ did shed His tear.

"You loved but one, and he unworthy, too;
How can you hope a crown to gain?
Congenial love, though's right, when nobly true—
The same through shadow, sun, or pain.
It brings the sweetest joys of earthly time,
And fills with sunshine, all its days;
When hearts are tuned to Love's sweet song and
rhyme—
Departing not from Honor's ways.

"This boon of love is woman's shield and life—
Her hope, her joy, her long sought prize—
And all that makes a good and happy wife—
The soul of beauty in her eyes.—
The bond that binds her loved one to the home—
That sweetly guards the spring of life—
That holds the children fast, from tempting
Rome,
Around the fireside, free from strife.

" 'Tis heaven's gift of bliss God willed to Eve
To make her life one lasting joy;
Were not she caught by Satan's lured deceive,
She yet would know no woes' annoy;
But now tis half and half, a smile, a tear—
A day of hope and cloudless blue—
A night of storm and gloom and living fear.—
A heart that's false, a heart that's true.

"First, woman fell by apples luscious red,
   And man was doomed by tempted share;
But lately, Satan tempts the man, instead,
   With wine-cup's ruddy, luring glare;
So man has caused the race a second fall,
   But woman bears its load of woe;
It kills her peace, and throws o'er love and all,
   A gloom that's worse than known before.

"To her is measured now more saddening care,
   Than peace and joy, and hours of rest;
More sleepless nights and heartless blows to bear,
   Than happy days with loved ones blest.
Our saving Christ was man's salvation, great,
   For all his fall from Eden's bliss;
But this last fall from grand manhood's estate,
   To darkest plains of sin, like this,"

"Will Prohibition from disgracing shame
   Soon come to make him free and wise?
It will refine his tarnished, rusting name,
   And open wide his heart and eyes.
Fair maid, cast off your badge of LOVE; go live
   For God and man, and truth and right,
And wear this badge of DUTY I now give;
   Your life will then be pure delight.

"List to the music sweet from Heaven's choir,
   Heed not the doleful strain, 'Regret';
Make love for all, your soul and heart's desire;
   Remember God, your lost forget,

For Prohibition work and fight and pray,
  And live to do your duty more;
And then, at last, when comes your dying day,
  We'll welcome you on Heaven's shore."

VIII.

The angel left her there alone to think—
  A noise! she looked—an army grand
Was marching straight to Death's cold river-
    brink.
  They stepped, "Columbia," by the band.
The soldiers wore a sad, expressive face,
  Which told of hopes long lost in gloom;
Of lives misspent, without one spark of grace—
  They seemed to know that next came doom.

They were striving to run far away from the
    river so cold,
But a general and thirty-eight captains, with
    officers bold,
  Were sufficient to keep sixty thousand at bay.
Lillie's wonder aroused, then she said · "What,
    kind stranger, can mean
All this numberless army that reaches as far as
    can be seen;
  Can it be that the world has been ended to-
    day?"

But as he turned to speak, a horrid fright
  Ran through her till her blood was cold.
In gilded letters, "WHISKY APPETITE,"
  He wore in front on badge of gold.
She looked 'round at the army; every man
Was cursed with this all-shameful, telling
    brand,
  Which showed that honor had been sold.

A shamed expression, from an unknown woe,
  Crept o'er the officer's rough face,
When first he saw fair Lillie's heavenly glow;
  Perchance, a thought of life's disgrace—
A thought of his own wife, once angel fair,
And all the pain he made her bear,
  But quick to answer he made haste:

"Fair maid, 'tis Whisky's annual army great,
That marches on to Hell these years of late;
  It's from United States alone.
The officers of my own rank you see,—
Our Captain State commissions us to be
  Lieutenant Rum Sellers at home.

"We have to pay our good old Captain State
To get this office—high with honor—great;
  But soon we make our money back.
We make our soldiers round us trembling stand,
And take from them their goods—to house and
    land—
  Captain don't care if they're beat black.

"There're forty-four, these Captain States, so
    grand;
They own the whole rich country, Unionland;
    But six are shabbiest men who live,
They never help to guide this army through,
But stay at home to make improvements new,
    And share the rest their labors give.

"That's General Samuel Union, greatest man
Who ever led the victory-gaining van;
    He gives to Satan, for some gold,
To keep his stately buildings and affairs
In goodly fix and give them kingly airs;—
    Satan steals it from him, we're told."

"This army, sixty thousand men, so brave,
Are marched to Hell each year, by way of
    Grave;
    They volunteered where whisky sold."
He would have said mu.h more, but proud
    command,
"In file, march into river, every man!"
    But horrors! what did she behold?

The star-decked flag, our country's precious boon,
    The heritage of Freedom's fight,
The general waved, alas! so deadly soon
    'Twould go into the land of night.
Impulsive thrill! she bound, the flag to save,
And cried: "Traitor! betraying, wretched
    knave!
    How dare you sell our country's right?"

But no, her weakly hands could not regain
   The flag, the gift from Honor's will.
The general, heartless wretch, with mind insane,
   Then fiercely struck the maid, until
She fell, heartbroken, on the slippery ground,
Amid the scoffs and sneers of all around.
   The general said, in harshest thrill:

"Take that, unwoman thing! and leave for home,
   Where all your kind should have to stay,
And when you learn some sense, you'll let alone
   Us men, who have the right to say
And do what we think best for country's good.
The men are they who have to gain a liveli-
     hood,
   And always will have their own way."

Though stung by these rough words, and hurt
    by blow,
   The savage general had just dealt;
Forgot she all she had to undergo,
   And only for the banner felt:—
"If I were now a man," the heroine said,
"I'd save my country's flag, or fall here dead;
   I'd save the land where Freedom dwelt.

"God curse the soul that is so wretched low
   To sell our Liberty, we prize
Above all else earth's longing mortals know,
   The best and sweetest boon that lies

Within the reach of man. It gives a peace
That's only known to souls when chains release,
To let them roam 'neath home's blue skies.

"Traitor! can you forget what blood has
    bought—
That Revolution fathers spilled?—
The liberty for which Washington fought,
    And to our nation's trust was willed?
The flag that waved in triumph for the Right—,
Can you take down in Hell's abyss of night,
    To wave no more o'er hearts it thrilled?"

Still on they go as heedless as a stone,
    As heartless as a time-worn tree;
A prayer she cries, with a despairing moan:—
    "Will crime triumph o'er bended knee?
God! can the flag that waved o'er land and sea
Be torn from hands and hearts of brave and
    free?
O God send help! I trust in thee!"

Behind a rush! she heard a running man
    Leap by. He grasped the flag to save;
He triumphed soon and bore from Satan's van—
    Yes, from the clench of savage knave,
The precious flag of downtrod, fallen right.
Bold Lillie's face then beamed with heav'nly light,
    When conquered this hero so brave.

Impulse o'erwhelmed, at once she ran to meet,
To welcome, love, and learn the name
Of this fair model hero, brave and fleet,
A man who'll have no peer in fame.
He smiled and said his name was Prohibition,
His work to better fallen man's condition—
To keep him from dread whisky's flame.

His features were as fair as the sun in the
morning,
And his eyes were so kind and so tenderly blue,
Much intelligence beaming, his face was adorning,
And to honor and duty he lived to be true.
On his brow the word GOD in bright gold was
gleaming,
In his hands, the dear flag of our country, he
bore,
O'er his heart, the sweet letters of HOME were
gleaming.—
He was purest of mortals that dwelt here
below.

Our true Lillie was beaming with lovelit glowing,
And her feelings were opened with wishes for
him :—
"May the breezes of heaven fore'er be blowing
O'er the land that's honored with your home
—a love hymn.

"May the whispers of peace and the music of
Heaven
Ever echo their joys o'er the loved of your
home;
May the smiles of prosperity and hope be given
To the firesides of all in the country you roam.

"May you guard the motto of HOME you're
bearing;
May you treasure the trust of the banner you
wave,
May the sons of freedom forever be sharing
All 'the land of the free and the home of the
brave;'
May the stars of that flag for men's rights be
shining,
May the rivers of love forever overflow,
May the blessings of God, all your days be lining,
May you reign King of Home, till you're called
from below."

"Lovely maid, take the thanks that my tongue
can't express;
Ever on through my life, will the prayers you
have said,
Be a solace and cheer that my memory will bless.
Like a prophet, my hopes and my aims you
have read;

'Tis for freedom, my country, full justice and
    right,—
  'Tis for home and its sacred love shrine which
    God gave,
That forever I'll stand and there bravely will
    fight
  Till King Whisky is killed, and Love's banner
    can wave.

"Noble maid, for your work and your prayers
    for me,
  I will guard and will keep all your loved ones
    from fear,
Woman's dower I'll bring to the homes of the
    free—
  The sweet dower of love, and protection so
    dear.
To the firesides I'll give the contentment of bliss,
  A sweet haven of rest—a long reign of loved
    peace—
Tender smilings of love—holy virtue's own kiss—
  All of these, I'll bring that woman's joys may
    increase.

All the men will be gallant, kind-hearted, and
    true;
  They will carry the banner of honor and right,
I will make them so loving and noble for
    woman's trust due,
  That no heart will be wrecked with neglect,
    nor with blight.

"All the land soon will grow and will prosper in
   wealth,
   And the South and the North and the East
      and the West
Will be free from vile liquor's devastating
   stealth.
   Then the homes and the nation and all will be
      blest.

"And no more will the lover be drawn by the
   snare,
   From the heart and the side of his darling
      sweet Love,
And no longer will maid have to pine and to bear,
   For the loved and the lost till death calls her
      above.
But her love will be true and her days will be
   blest
   With the bounty of home and its pleasures
      untold,—
With companionship sweet of her dearest and
   best,
   'Twill return all the bliss of the Eden of old."

Lillie's eyes then were sparkling with hopefulness
   bright,
   And they showed that a gloom had just passed
      far away,
As her blue orbs then beamed with a glorious
   light,
   While she looked him the thanks that her
      tongue could not say.

"God bless you," she murmured, as he bade her
   good-bye:
"I'm content now to live for my duty to him,
Ne'er again shall I utter a moan or a sigh,
   For my lost, though the light in my heart
   groweth dim."

IX.

The vision faded, 'twas a fevered dream
Of how she tried to cross life's darksome stream.
   She then awoke to feel her pain;
But every hour would bring a brighter glow,
Till soon her body strong did health bestow:
   The smile of peace came home again.

Long, weary days of death her love had fraught,
But still the badge of DUTY, good, it bought:
   That made her woe bring heav'nly peace;
Would we could blindly trust in God, with faith,
And lean on what the sacred scripture saith,
   Then joy and right would e'er increase.

Each cheering, rosy morn, with brush unseen,
Which painted all the sylvan woods so green,
   Would gently touch sweet Lillie's cheek,
Until it shone again with beauty rare,
And graced with Duty's peace and virtue's fair.
   Sweet mercy's light beamed round her feet.

Quite soon she walked those old remembered
  ways,
And sang again the memory 'chanted lays;
  Then oft an unknown woe would rise,
And bring a lonely tear of vague regret—
A wish that Love and she had never met
  With bliss and grief, and joy and sighs.

Oh, memory! why renew thy backward flight
To foolish days of love, that turned to night?
  Why keep us doomed to live the past?—
It has no peace, that's free from longing woe—
It's all a seeming charm of distant glow—
  A siren dream that does not last.

Why shun the present day with all its store,
And run to ope the luring memory door.
  Oh, mortal! live God's given time.
But if no star will send its cheering light,
And all your present lot is gloomy night,
  Then live in Hope, the land of rhyme.

But if this land is turned to burning waste,
Then welcome Christ; He'll make your heart
    more chaste,
  And give you Duty's badge and boon.
Then friends will come and heaven's blessings
    greet;
The birds will sing; the land will seem more
    sweet;
  On every knoll, a flower will bloom.

These noble thoughts would cross her mind, and
    oft
They'd bring a balmy, soothing music soft
    With tones of consolation dear.
And then she'd think no more of Love's star set,
But look at Duty's brighter star she'd met,
    Which sent its cheering beams so near.

X.

‚She wrote to her loved John, though lost, still
    dear.
He held the trusted post of engineer.
    She sent him Fate's unchanging will.
As parting keepsake from her heart and soul,
She wrote two poems for his good to toll,
    When tempting snares would lure to ill:—

THE RAILROAD OF LIFE.

This life is like a crooked railroad;
    The engineer is brave,
Who makes the rough, long trip successful
    From Cradle to the Grave.

And there are many stations on it,—
    On this railroad of life;
False flags will wave to stop your engine
    And plunge it into strife,

And you may run the curves of trouble;
   For days and nights with ease;
But time will have you side-tracked,
   By the switchman, Disease.

And you may cross the plains of manhood,
   Run tunnels long of strife,
But having God as your conductor
   On lightning train of life,

You'll never have to fear the stitching,
   On up-grades 'long the road.
If you have Hope for your good fireman,
   You'll always pull the load.

Now name your engine, True Religion,
   While running day or night;
And use the coal of Faith for fuel—
   'Twill always run you right.

Then never falter in your duty,
   But put your trust in him,
And you will always find your engine
   In best of running trim.

Always be mindful of instruction—
   Your duty never lack;
Still keep your hand upon the throttle—
   Your eye upon the track.

But you will often find obstruction
   That's laid by evil brain
Across some dangerous, frightful chasm,
   To try to wreck your train.

Then stop and move the dreadful danger,
   Then mount and onward go;
Still put your trust in Christ, the Savior,
   Vile plans He'll overthrow.

Then ring your bell and blow your whistle,
   Let not your courage slack;
E'er keep your hand upon throttle,
   Your eye upon the track.

When you have made the trip successful,
   And at your journey's end;
You'll find the blessed angels waiting
   To welcome you right in.

And then you will meet the Superintendent,
   Who's waiting for you now,
With blissful, happy smiles of welcome—
   A crown to deck your brow.

("The Railroad of Life" was really written by the heroine.)

REMEMBER ME AND SHUN THE BOWL.

Fate has parted us forever,
    Untuned our harps of music sweet;
Gone, the days of love and pleasure,
    Their smiles no more our hearts will see.
Satan lured you from my keeping,
    And bound to Demon Drink, your soul—
Stealing all that's pure and holy—
    Remember me, and shun the bowl.

Has your manhood passed away,
    Has courage left a weakly hand?
Be a hero now of valor,
    The hellish drink and snare withstand;
Temperance, truth, and virtuous living,
    Are names on Honor's manhood roll,
Heed the cry of loving Lillie,—
    Remember me, and shun the bowl.

Think of your dear saintly mother,
    Who's praying God her son to save;
Soon, if you don't change for better,
    You'll send her hopeless to the grave.
Think of your lost darling Lillie,
    Who loved you from her heart and soul;
Think of how you sent the sorrow—
    Remember me, and shun the bowl.

Think of your dear loving sister,
    Now budding fair with rosy bloom—
Think—a drunkard might be wooing,
    To fill her life with endless doom.
Cries she oft, to know you're drinking;
    It wounds her very inmost soul.
Think of all the woe you're causing;
    Remember me, and shun the bowl.

Painful tears are quickly running
   Down o'er the cheeks that once you kissed;
But 'tis vain to be repining
   For all the joy our love has missed;
John, grant me one farewell favor,
   It comes from out my heart and soul;
Do whate'er you will, but always
Remember me, and shun the bowl !

LILLIE.

These verses, covered o'er with spots of tears,
   She sent as farewell warning's call
To him who brightened all her sunny years—
   First love—last love—that tells it all.
She begged him then to go so far away,
   Their eyes would never meet again,
Until beyond the final judgment day
   They met above life's ruining gin.

At once John —— left his post as engineer;
   And none has known, yet, where he went;
Inquired and searched, have people, far and near,
   But never news from him was sent.
Young man! launched out on vice and luring
      snares,
   Bereft of hope and love and joy—
We send to God our earnest, pleading prayers—
   Lord, may he shun the drink's decoy.

XI.

If Lillie's mind were only highly trained
  In school, and on through college, too,
For tender verse and thoughts, she'd soon be
    famed
  Far more than poets which she knew.
"But Knowledge to her eyes, its ample page,
  Rich with the spoils of Time, did ne'er unroll;
Chill Penury repressed her noble rage,
  And froze the genial current of her soul."

But still despite her constant household care—
  Bereft of gentle word that flows
In milder streams from those who learning
    share—
Though still, her happy love in maiden youth—
  Her loss which willed the boon of Duty,
Did fill her soul with music, heav'n and truth,
  So that oft writes she verse of beauty :—

Dark and Bright.

No sweet hope lives, but what to-morrow,
  With cruelness and fears,
Will kill and bury long in sorrow,
  And cover o'er with tears.

There's not a plan but what will tumble
  And fall to depths below;
There's not a man but what will grumble,
  In this sad world of woe.

There's not a flow'r, but blooms to wither
    And live, no, nevermore;
There's not a friend, but wanders hither,
    Where we can never go.

There's not a soul that soars to glory,
    And shares all earthly fame;
But soon we'll cease to tell his story,
    And soon forget his name.

There's not a heart that shares Fruition—
    Desire will never cease;
Our hearts are prone to pain's condition,
    And never made for peace.

Our souls will never lose their longing,
    Our hearts, their aching pain,
Until we leave this land of wronging,
    And cross beyond life's main.

Yes, there's a home in distant Aidenn,
    Where live the pure and free—
A rest for souls with sorrow laden—
    A balm for you and me.

This home, with all the peaceful glory
    That bliss can sweetly give,
Is free to all who read its story,
    And ever faithful live.

Ah, now! I'll work alone for Duty—
    The good that I can do!
I'll leave the flaws and look for beauty
    And seek the smiles in view.

And now I find in life a pleasure—
On every face a smile;
In every heart a golden treasure,
Sweet peace lives all the while.

No flower withers, till another
Is born to bloom as fair;
No friend departs until some other
Is found our love to share.

No sweet hope lives but what to-morrow
Will roll its stone away;
No rending pain e'er reigns in sorrow,
But what will die some day.

To live for God and Man and Heaven,
All troubles pass away;
For then our lives are sweet with leaven,
Content then smiles each day.

"Full many a gem of rarest ray serene,
The dark, unfathomed caves of ocean bear—
Full many a flow'r is born to blush unseen,
And waste its sweetness on the desert air."

If the flow'rs from the wildwood and jewels
from sea,
Could be gathered, what beautiful garlands
would be!
If the flowers of mind and the jewels of soul,
Could be gathered on earth, we would have
Heaven's whole.

Under Liberty's throne and Prosperity's home,
Far more flow'rs could be culled from the parch-
    ing dry loam;
But the strife's for the gold—not the bettering
    of mind,
Hence the many who have perished for tending,
    we find.

Alabama's responsible for ignorance of late,
That exists in our homes, more than in another
    State.
'Tis no wonder that Lillie's education was small,
As she lived behind Poverty's dark, heavy wall;
For her father, a farmer, with family large,
Had a struggling hard work to support well his
    charge.
And the public free schools for three months and
    some less,
Were all out by the time that a child could
    progress.

But boys of high ambition, joined to pluck,
Have overcome and blessed all this bad luck.
They work and go to school, then work again,
Until at last they're great and able men.
If any man deserve our highest praise,
'Tis he who climbs from Poverty's dark ways.
This is the reason why that "Here we rest,"
Has men that grand Nobility counts best.

But her neglect to educate the poor,
Has made her ballot more corrupt than sure;
Her institutions, too, will stay on sand,
Unless the children now in her command,
Are taught and trained for citizenship true.
As it has been, no difference what they do,
The girls can never rise as boys have done.
It surely is a partial luck for one.

So girls with fathers poor, have had to pine
And live without the cultures that refine.
If Mercy's balm e'er soothe a human breast,
It should be girls by hope and want oppressed.
Oh! noble hope that burns the livelong day!
Will man e'er roll the heavy stone away?
It is a cowardly, unmanly sin
To keep them doomed e'er with "It might have
    been."

I crave to be a wealthy millionaire
For only this; when girls are found so rare,
To open doors for hopes that ever cling,
And help them mount to learning's sweet'ning
    spring.
Oh, woman pure! if earth have long oppressed,
God gives a home where you will e'er be blest.
No hopes there wail, no loved one proves untrue.
There brightest stars will shine in crowns for
    you.

But there is always a befitting place,
By God ordained, for humblest one of race.
"Work for some good, be it ever so slowly,
Cherish some flower, be it ever so lowly,
Labor! all labor is noble and holy!"
So Duty found for Lillie many ways,
Despite her chance, where weakly hand e'er pays,
And soon her influence, good, around her sways.

She visits sick and seems to them as sent,
Like angels, with the balm of sweet content.
And ev'ry Sunday morning bright,
She's at her Sabbath-school class; blessed sight,
To see her teach the little children how to live
To share the glor'ous peace that Christ can give.
And soon the trusting ones have learned to love,
And think her sweet and pure as gentle dove.

XII.

The noblest work she yet has ever done—
  One that will win a heav'n and a crown:—
The friendship of the village girls she won.—
  Her gracious influence circling round
Them for the holy temperance cause to strive
  And work to drive all whisky from the place.
The village once was beautiful and live
  With every good and chastening grace.

Its rural people then were richly blest
  With love and honor, health and ease.
Contented hours, in plenty, then were dressed,
  And peaceful pleasures came to please.
Sweet maidens, rosy-cheeked and angel-fair,
  Once wandered o'er the village green.
They beamed with virtue's holy smile so rare—
  No lovelier, happier girls were seen.

Their health and beauty, full of nature's grace,
  No fashion craze had yet oppressed.
The mother's care—the father's pride, no race
  With sweeter girls were ever blest.
The boys grew honest, kind, and true;
  A Christian training brightly shone
From handsome brows which plainly showed
    they'd do
  To enter noble work when grown.

School buildings—churches, crowned the rising
    hills,
  Where happy, Christian people, true
To God and home and native land, instilled
  The worth of mind and heart, all through
The glowing youthful years, to children dear.
Alas! they dreamed not then, a frowning day
  Of vice quite soon would reign supreme,
And that the dear ones that they taught with
    fear
  Would soon be turned to wretches mean.

A railroad soon ran 'cross the village green,
  'Twas welcomed with a cheering gieet,
For then the busy world could e'er be seen—
  New styles and ways were thought so sweet.
The boys then went to cities large,
  And to the railroad with its snares.
The honest looks and virtuous ways, encharged
  To them at fireside evening prayers,

Saloons and wicked comrades, round their vine
  Of luscious temperance fruit, home gave,
Ere long the once so noble sons, entwine
  Their necks with chains to drunkard's graves.
Oh, world of change! what can an hour bring?—
  A grief for joy—a wreck for man,
A hell for home—a woe for mother's sting.
  The village was by drink o'erran,

The churches lost their glow of heavenly white
  And plainly showed there was neglect;
The schoolhouse caught the deadly rusting
    blight,
  Its former glory soon was wrecked.
O God! can't love its rural kingdom hold,
  Its village home of blessed peace,
Where virtue's mint yields pure and lasting gold
  And sinless pleasures ne'er decrease;

But social hours of joy and merry song,
And gatherings at the day's decline,
Gave way for dancing all the night-time long,
And constant revels in the wine.
The maids have lost their winsome beauty fair,
That queenly face that won the heart;
They're nothing now but giddy girls who share
No charms that womanhood impart.

These girls that used to ply the household care,
And let their mothers have some rest,
Now lounge, and read the trashy novel's snare,
And let alone the books which blessed
Their growing minds and hearts in days gone by.
Their mothers bear the burden now,
While daughters frolic, fret, and wish, and sigh
For stylish dress and paint for brow.

No worthy, manly men now come to woo
And win a queen to bless a home,
But dudes and flirts and drinking boys, untrue—
They promise city homes and latest style,
And ne'er will let them work again,
Girls yield with pride, but ere a little while,
They're lost to peace by worthless men.

XIII.

Such havoc wild, the drink fiend wrought for
   years,
   Until bold Lillie came to save.
The girls she told of whisky's killing tears,
   That lead our loved ones to the grave;
She told of liquor's wrongs too long endured,
   Of how the village used to be—
She mentioned sacred rights to be secured
   Before their hearts from grief would free.

She worked with faithful, patient efforts long,
   And got the girls quite all agreed
To shun, and ne'er respect, like shameful wrong,
   The men who're bound to whisky's greed.
She wakened slumbering right, and taught a
   truth
   That they who countenance a vice,
Are sinners, too; 'tis true from age to youth,
   In all the actions that entice.

The ladies, who associate with men
   Of dissipated habits vile,
Are great accessories to help the sin
   Of drink to spread and more beguile.
The worthless "gentlemen"(?) then raved and
   swore
   That soon the "saints" would welcome them,
And said the town was dead to live no more—
   The worst then left for darker den.

Ere long the better sons and fathers true,
   Are roused from honor's shameful sleep,
And organize a Prohibition crew,
   And work with might and main to keep
Saloons and whisky men from out the town;
   Quite soon their efforts paid full well,
For now no whisky hells are close around—
   No place for vice and crime to dwell.

The golden days then slowly come again,
   But healing sores ne'er lose their scars:—
Mothers knew not the peace that once had been—
   Some sons behind the prison bars!
Some daughters now are drunkard's wives,
      bereft
   Of all the peace a home can give,
Their hope, their joy, their peace, their all, was
      left
   To sink where lasting miseries live.

But still the palmy days of old renewed
   And sweetened hearts that lived regret;
Then sunshine, progress, peace, and love ensued—
   A heav'nlier change was never met.
All praise to Lillie, her'ine for the Right,—
   An angel sent for home's defense;
Would there were thousands such to use their
      might,
   Constructing, 'round the home, a fence.

Some years rolled by, the village prospered well;
  As fruits of peace and love and truth,
A high-school building stood with merry bell
  To call aspiring, happy youth.
And Lillie's father, true to parents' due,
  Then left the farm, by riverside,
And moved his family to the village, too;
  Where they did pleasantly reside,

While all his children to the growing school,
  Then went and learned so very fast;
They loved their teachers and obeyed their rule,
  Till happy school-days, all were past.
Oh! how they love their father, kind and dear,
  For doing this for their own sake,—
To leave the farm and move so very near,
  Then work—while they their schooling take.

Such noble fathers, e'er will children bless
  By word and then by living creed;
They'll emulate their christianlike goodness,
  And live to work for honor's need.
From homes like this come those who bless the
    race—
  Self-made—they tempered their own steel;
They're firm and true and e'er will bravely face
  The foe, for right and country's weal.

The worthy father toiled from morn till night;
Through sun and rain, through heat and cold,
Until his constitution broke outright,
And soon for him the church bell tolled!
Heartrending grief long flows when rich men
die
And leave their loved ones, money's wealth;
But think how hard must be the painful cry,
When poor men die, and leave to stealth,

Their families large, with nothing to sustain!
His only son was scarce fourteen—
Ah! picture grief, and hope decayed to pain!
And children robbed of vernal green!
The children one short year in school had spent—
Now all their chance to learn seemed past;
And worse than all, their hearts were sorely
rent—
Sad gloom their days had overcast.

'Twas all that could be done by them to earn,
While their dear father was alive,
A common living, by an economic turn,
But now they must still harder strive.
Good Lillie helped her mother all the year,
To let her sisters go to school;
Ah! 'twould have been a privilege so dear,
Could she have gone to learning's yule.

And still a heroine, she proved to be,
  In this dark hour of want and woe;
She and her little brother worked so free,
  That no great want the family knew;
She and a younger sister clerked in store,
  Her brother hired in various ways;
The younger girls were sent to school some more,
  Heroic work, like this, we praise!

XIV.

Two years roll by—her father had just bought
  Their village home before he died,
But had not paid for it; so, when 'twas sought,
  They could no longer there abide.
So, to the little farm, again they moved;
  'Twas hard to leave the village dear,
And part with those whom friendship had im-
    proved.
  But still it was so very near,

That oft the boys and girls would spend
  A pleasant day at Lillie's home;
A merry time, the day would always send,
  While 'mong the river flowers they roam.
Out in the swift canoe, they joyous glide,
  And fish and talk the hours away; ·
Such country pleasures, that to some denied,
  Make glad the hours a lonely day.

'Twas here I met the lovely heroine true—
The heroine for Duty's might;
She made me turn for Prohibition, new—
To stand for home and country's right.
Her pure, sweet Christian life, and works sub-
lime,
Have sent God's sunshine to my heart;
Such virtuous maidens sweeten earth's lone clime
With smiling sunshine they impart.

On lightning wheels, the years are rolling by—
They all find Lillie true to right;
Her badge of Duty, ne'er will she deny,
Its radiance gives a gracious light;
Full many men of honor came to woo
And win the lovely heroine;
But to her lost—her only Love—she's true,
Her heart echoes: "It might have been."

The cheerful morning-glory vine,
Round her cottage porch doth twine;
Cool zephyrs, from the river sent,
Are laden with a sweet content;
Though yet she hears the strain, "Regret,"
And sighs that Hope's loved star has set,
Ere long, she'll bud and sweetly bloom
In Aidenn spring, beyond the tomb.

PART III.

ALABAMA WRITERS.

It was the worthy aim of the author to introduce, through this part, every Alabama writer of note and merit. But with his short acquaintance with the *literati* of the State, and his limited time in preparing this, he fears that many who deserve a notice have not been represented. It was his object to introduce each one by an acrostic, followed by the best thoughts to be culled from his or her respective writing; but want of space, time, and an opportunity to select from the writing of every one, has prevented this being done in every case.

Truly, Alabama should feel proud of her writers, and considering the number of her promising young authors, she, perhaps, soon, will hold the front rank in Southern letters.

Father Abram J. Ryan, formerly of Mobile, was the warmest patriotic poet of the South. Mrs. Augusta Evans Wilson, now living in Mobile, is one of the greatest of novel writers. There is a strain of nobleness and purity of sentiment pervading her numerous works. Judge A. B. Meek, who died at the close of the war, in Tuscaloosa, was an uncommonly sweet poet. He published two books of poems; both are out of print now.

One was entitled "Songs and Poems of the South."
Dr. Samuel Minturn Peck, of Tuscaloosa, is in
many respects the greatest living poet. He would
be known and loved in every cultured home in our
Southland, but his verses are copyrighted by a
Northern publisher and, consequently, not so extensively sold in the South. The author is indebted
to the kindness of Fredrick A. Stokes & Co., New
York, for the privilege of selecting the roses of
thought from his second volume of poems, "Rings
and Love Knots." The young and wonderfully
gifted Miss Ruby Beryl Kyle, of Birmingham, has
made a brilliant debut into the world of letters,
as a story-writer and the author of "Paul St.
Paul." The South learned with pride of the
marvelous genius of Miss Alice Vivian Brownlee,
of Mulberry, who, at the age of fifteen, had written the delightfully sweet and tender novel, "The
Affinities," for the copyright of which she refused
$2,800. Dr. Orion T. Dozier, in his recent book of
poems, "Foibles of Fancy and Rhymes of the
Times," has given our patriotic literature an
offering to make us admire him and love him.
Miss Mary Gordon Duffee, of Blount Springs, has
long been giving to the world the fruits of her re-
markable genius for poetry and history. Mrs. B.
F. Moore, of Auburn, has been delighting the
humorous world with the backwoods sketches of
"Betsy Hamilton." Mr. Aubrey Harwell, of
Birmingham, is a sweet and promising singer.
Miss Margaret O'Brien, of Birmingham, is a rare

writer. Mr. T. C. DeLeon, of Mobile, is a worthy contributor of the *Century Magazine*. Miss Veni McDonald ("Pearl Meredyth") has, from early childhood, been giving us rare, sweet thoughts in story and verse. Dr. J. M. P. Otts, of Greensboro, is a talented theological and Biblical writer. Mrs. J. I. McKenney, of Montgomery, some years ago, published a creditable volume of verses under the pseudonym, "Katy-did." Mr. J. Burdick Clarke, of Montgomery, is an interesting dialect story-writer. Mr. J. Waller Henry, of Montgomery, writes beautiful poems. Mrs. Zula B. Cook, of Anniston, and Mrs. Mary Ware, of Birmingham, have appreciated poems published frequently.

Among other writers are Mrs. Alice Kate Roland, Birmingham; Mrs. Francis Jansenius, Birmingham; Prof. S. L. Robertson, Birmingham; Mr. T. M. Owen, Birmingham; Mr. Sheffield (deceased), Bessemer; Mr. John E. Brady ("Joe Archy"), Bessemer; Rev. J. L. Abernathy, Langston; Miss Martha Young ("Eli Shepheard"), Greensboro; Mrs. J. B. Lennard ("Evola"), Wilson Ridge; and Miss Sallie Oden, Bangor.

Those whom the author has not mentioned have not been neglected intentionally, but for want of their acquaintance.

Southern breezes rose and milder blew,
As, when out the gates 'neath heaven's bow'rs,
Minturn, through the ether wavelets flew
Unto our sweet summer land of flow'rs.
Empyrean songs from courts of blue
Lent glad melodies to be his dow'rs.

Mantled with the South's fond bending skies,
Idolized with cool magnolia's shade,
Nursed mid flow'rs as fair as sunset dyes,
'Tis no wonder he has gladly made
Unto song the wealth of all his ties.
Purer, sweeter gems, with Muses' aid,
Never from a genius soul did rise!

Poet-laureate of gentler rhymes!
Each quaint song of innocence and glee
Calls an honor to our Southern climes—
Known his fame across the barrier sea.

(RINGS AND LOVE KNOTS.)

The mocking bird joined in my reckless glee,
  I longed for no angel's wing,
I was just as near Heaven as I wanted to be
  Swinging in the grapevine swing.
I'm tired of the world with its pride and pomp
  And fame seems a worthless thing.
I'd barter it all for one day's romp,
  And a swing in the grapevine swing.
  Swinging in the grapevine swing,
  Laughing where the wild birds sing,
      I would I were away
      From the world to-day,
  Swinging in the grapevine swing.

      ————

      She hath a witching dimple;
        Now was it not a sin
      That when the fairies crowned her
        They put that dimple in!
      The heartaches it hath given
        It grieves my soul to think;
      She has no care how lovers fare—
        The little lass in pink.

      ————

Meet me where the apple blossoms blow;
  Let the floating petals flake your tresses,
Breathing us a benison below,
  Crowning our betrothal with caresses.
      For in the upper deep,
      The stars are now a-peep,

The drowsy river murmurs in its flow,
I hear its voice repeating:
"Life's in blossom—time is fleeting."
Ah! let us catch the fragrance ere it go,
Love
Oh,
Meet me where the apple-blossoms blow!

The love in my heart is as strong as the hills
And as deep as the fathomless sea,
Yet pure as the breath of the rose that thrills
The soul of the summer with glee.
As fair as the light of the faithful stars
That beam in the boundless blue;
No selfish mote its radiance mars,
And sweetheart, it is all for you.
All for you!
Strong and true,
No time the tie can sever,
Till the angels doubt,
And the stars burn out,
I am yours, sweetheart, forever.

Chrysanthemums are fair,
And orchids are rare,
And many there be that love them!
But with dew-besprinkled faces,
And wildwood graces;
Oh, the blackberry blossoms are above them!

So, loyal little rosebud,
Just whisper to my sweet;
  I sigh for her,
  I'd die for her,
My heart is at her feet.

———

What were life without you, Oh, I cannot, dare
  not dream!
'Twere worthless as a shattered leaf upon an autumn stream!
    O my sweet,
    At your feet,
      Heed my lonely cry;
    Grant relief
    To my grief,
      Love me, or I die!

———

I've toiled and won an honored name,
  And now I'm growing old;
I've touched the shining hem of fame,
  And found its touch was cold;
But still, from out the shadowy past,
  One memory brings me bliss,
For I shall keep, while life shall last,
  Our first betrothal kiss.

Her breath is like the breeze that plays
Amid the fragrant thorn ;
Her voice outsweets the rill that strays
Through April woods at morn.
Alas! for him who stops to gaze
Upon her locks a-twined;
His aimless feet shall go their ways,
And leave his heart behind.

———

If on the field of love you fall,
With smiles conceal your pain ;
Be not to love too sure a thrall,
But lightly wear his chain.
Don't kiss the hem of Beauty's gown,
Or tremble at her tear,
And when caprices weigh you down,
A word within your ear:
Another lass, another lass,
With laughing eyes and bright—
Make love to her,
And trust me, sir,
'Twill set your wrongs aright.

———

O little love, with wayward curls,
No jewel do I bring you;
If tripping rhymes were glossy pearls,
What shining gems I'd string you!
And through the night,
With laughing light,
A diadem I'd fling you.

Senorita, dark thy hair,
  Gleaming with imprisoned light,
Like a subtle shining snare,
  Tangling fast my dreams by night.
Sleep or waking, still for thee,
  All my fevered thoughts do flow;
Sweetheart, if thou lov'st not me,
  Break the spell and let me go.

Our love-life has witnessed more laughing than
    weeping;
  We chase with fond kisses the footprints of care;
But my little wife never dreams I am keeping
  The little red ribbon she wore in her hair,
    Though faded and crinkled,
    And rumpled and wrinkled,
  The bonnie bright looping that glistened so fair;
    Far down in my pocket
    It lies in a locket,
  The little red ribbon she wore in her hair.

Oh! could some painter's facile brush,
On canvas limn my garden's blush,
The fevered world its din would hush
  To crown the high endeavor;
Or could a poet snare in rhyme
The breathings of this balmy clime,
His fame might dare the dart of Time
  And soar undimmed forever!

She sings as soft as the wind that grieves
When the summer roses blight.

O first love, O last love,
Beside the summer sea;
As clasps the wave the star above,
So clings my heart to thee!

Whose are the veins that laugh and leap,
Whenever thy name is heard?
Whose are the eyes that fain would weep,
To think of a hope deferred?
Whose is the arm that will not fail,
If ever thy need shall be?
Whose is the love that never grows pale?
Come, look in my heart, and see;
Dear heart,
Look in my heart and see.

Be my fate or dear or bright,
Soon, ah! soon I'll know it,
If I may not be her knight,—
Still I'll be her poet!

She stooped and plucked a daisy,
To bind amid her hair,
And I seemed to see it laughing
With the rapture to be there.

Wooing, wooing, wooing! Alas 'tis growing late
The birds are mated long ago; sweetheart shall
we not mate?
The tender melody of love makes music in the
blood;
The magic tide that comes but once is rolling to
the flood.
Alas! for those who dream and dream unplighted
on the shore,
And wake to find the tide of love has ebbed forevermore!

There was envy in the skies
When the stars beheld her eyes,
So lovely are the glances of that little lass of mine.
There's a song most wonderful that never has
been sung,
'Tis waiting for a worthy bard to breathe its
golden line;
O poet, come and sing it on a harp with silver
strings,   ,
No other lay were fitting for that little lass of
mine.
Come ripple forth the praises
Like the rillet through the daisies,
And let your rhymes part, meet and kiss like
blossoms on a vine,
While a fairy's wings unseen
Float the trembling strings between,
To make the carol meeter for that little lass of
mine.

(THE SOUTH.)

No blot of shame thy record mars
In senate-hall or lurid fight;
Thy spotless fame shines like the stars
That guard thee through the balmy night.
In weary wandering to and fro,
Thou hast my heart where'er I go.

And I dream by the billows blue
Of a heart that was leal and true;
And I vow by the tide,
Though fate may divide
My faith shall abide
And grow;
And my heart ever turn while the light stars burn
To my love in the long ago.

There is a mate for every heart
That throbs beneath the sun,
Though some by fate are kept apart
Till life is nearly done;
Where is the loyal heart and hand
Shall make my life complete?
God bless my love, on sea or land,
Until our paths shall meet!

Obedient fame to thoughts of birth divine,
Responds to meed the burning glow of thine.
In patriot hearts where live the inner soul
Of Southern hope, bulwarked with valor bold,
No song of thine will ever be untold.

Thy "Galaxy of Southern Heroes" brave,
Holds deathless tributes which vicious grave
Entombs not, while proud memory has a thought
Of how our Southern heroes braved and fought!
Put this beside the "Conquered Banner" grand!
Hold them to show the greatness of our land.
Impulsive with a patriot's burning zeal;
Luxuriant thoughts and wisdom's words of steel,
Unite to form a power of mighty name,
So strong and rich it wins thee peerless fame.

Descends thou then to milder, gentler strains
Of constant friendship, love, and their refrains.
Zeal's patriot poet, friendship's nobleman!
In loving fondness gentle zephyrs fan
Each treasured song of thine along the strand
Round Dixie's glorified immortal land.

11

154

("Foibles of Fancy and Rhymes of The Times.")

Let angels that hover around us in air,
  Keeping record of joys that bloom in the heart,
Proclaim from their tablets the dearest joy there;
  And in whispers of spirit we'll hear them impart,
That it is the sweet pleasures when exiles we roam,
  Of knowing that loved ones remember us still,
And that dear ones we've left behind us at home
  Have thoughts of ourselves, their memories to
    fill!

———

To flatter her is just as silly,
As trying to paint the fairest lily.

———

But I will not attach a blame
  To one of such transcendent charms;
For heaven itself would blush in shame
  To see such beauty in my arms.
'Twas fate that taught my youthful heart,
  Its love upon such charms to set,
But fate can never teach the art
  To change from love, and then forget.

———

When lips to lips and breast to breast
  In tenderness of love are pressed,
There speaks a voice from out the heart
That faltering words will not impart!
  And love's sweet music, through the voice
  Makes all within the soul rejoice!

And now all the joy in life that I ask
  Is to walk and to muse by the sea,
Whose every low surge is a funeral dirge
  For that loved one now lost to me.
And to gaze o'er the main with longings in vain,
  And to mingle my tears with the wave
Which the tides in their sweep shall bear o'er the
    deep,
  To moisten the grass on her grave.

    It is your promise to be mine,
      That like some sweet refrain
    Will echo in my heart
      Till I come back again.

    And oft when I in slumbers lie,
      My soul escaping from my breast,
    Will back to Minnie swiftly fly
      And vigils keep while she's at rest.

Oh, what in this life is worth living for me
When thy face and thy form no longer I see!
No music can soothe me, no pleasures delight,
When thou art not near me, my life is a blight!

    Then sitting down by Eula's side,
      I clasp her little hand in mine,
    And while the moments swiftly glide
      I drink the nectar—love divine!

Go search the world from pole to pole,
 And view mankind in every state;
You'll never find a living soul,
 Whate'er his land whate'er his fate,
Who has not felt within his breast
 The tides of sorrow ebb and flow,
And has not felt, when cares oppressed,
 That mortal man was made for woe.

   ———

And since to earth this queen was born,
 The ranks of beauty to adorn,
With every year more fair she's grown,
 Till I have vowed that little elf
Shall rule but one, and one alone,
 And I shall be that one myself.

   ———

And thus my joy in life shall be
 Whilst memory's chain holds firm and true;
Altho' your face no more I see,
 To sweetly—sweetly think of you.

   ———

Her lovely cheeks are soft and fair.
 As ever claimed a poet's thoughts.

   ———

My life is like a ship at sea
 That soon will sink beneath the wave,
And sinking leave no sigh or trace
 Of its eternal resting grave.

Old Satan never smiles so bright,
  Nor darker gloams the frowning skies,
Than when men split the right in twain
  And called the action "compromise."

And in the fields of human life,
  Oft found in humble ways
The pure in heart, the mild, and good
  Escape our upward gaze.
And in our rush and wild pursuit
  Of best in social skies,
We sometimes crush a noble breast
  That heaven itself would prize.

And when you go to church
  And sit down in er pew,
And a gal with monster hat
  Shuts the preacher out from view;
Don't you feel more like cussin'
  Than you do to kneel and pray,
Now, really, if you don't,
  Don't you sorter feel that way.

And you who's fond ob smokin',
  May put dis in yer pipe,
Dat a kicker am a greener
  Who's seldom ober ripe.

'Tis said that wicked Birmingham
  Is not a friend to grace;
That every dweller in its bounds
  Is heading for that place
Where waterworks are never known
  And ice supplies are scant,
But I don't think it wholly true,
  I can't, oh, I can't!

I don't go much on brag and blow
  And all dat kind ob stuff
But when it comes to what I no
  I guess I noes enuff;
I've read the Bible tru and tru
  And Watson's commontater
And what I hasn't got from books
  Ise learned from human nater.

My belubbed cullud brudders
  Havin' lef at home my specks
I'll hav ter ax yer pardin'
  Fer not readin' ob my tex;
But yer'll find de inspirasion
  Ob what I has ter say,
In the pistle ob de postle
  To de church in Africa.

My words are nuts o' wizdum,
  Shucked clean ob all de hulls,
And I hope dey'll find a lodgment
  In the hollers ob yer skulls.

Three cheers sed I fer that great man,
  Who allers holds his tung,
And never blows er bout a plan
  Till success ter it is brung.

(DUDE.)

I guess the God who made him
  Must have made him for a cause,
But really I'm too shallow
  To imagine what it was.
His head I know is empty,
  No virtue fills his breast,
And of all his mammy's children,
  He loves himself the best.

Yes, I rudder be er flyin' squirrel
  Ter fly erwhile and fall,
Dan ter be a lazy tarepin
  An' do nothin' else but crawl.

And I can't help hate a croaker,
  With his weak an' watery eyes,
Allers turned toward de groun',
  Neber raised toward de skies.

(GEORGIA.)

And thou hast many mountains grand
And valleys fair to see,
And Heaven's sun ne'er shone upon
A fairer land than thee;
And as thy wandering son returns,
Resolved no more to roam,
He lifts his song in measures strong
To praise his native home.

The banner of temperance now widely unfurled
Gives cheer to the nation and hope to the world.

But a calmness like that of a lake in a cave,
And a peace, undisturbed as the peace of the grave,
Shall reign o'er the land, and the country will
    seem
Like heavenly paradise viewed in a dream!

(TO FRANK STANTON.)

And love and tenderness and worth,
Like flowers that spring from mother earth,
Will ever bloom and bud and twine
Around the poet's sacred shrine;
And thy sweet songs, in sadness sung,
Shall live when death has stilled thy tongue.

Alabama! Alabama!
    I am dreaming now of thee,
And I see the trend of thousands,
    Coming from beyond the sea,
As they mount upon the billows,
    Streaming through the spray and foam
Wildly joyous of the prospect
    Of an Alabama home.
And I see within my dreaming,
    Visions of the future cast,
That shall overwhelm with brilliance
    All the glories of the past;
For I see the spirit, Progress,
    Hovering o'er thee with her wand,
At whose lightest touch, responding,
    Wonders burst on every hand.

And it may be in the future,
    Touched by Time's soft, soothing art,
That the blow will be forgotten,
    And love again revive her heart.

For never yet in any land,
    Was marshaled out a braver band
Than those who stood on Southern soil,
    To battle for their native land.

Fair sunny land—home of the brave,
  How wondrous and supremely blest!
Like billows on tempestuous sea,
  Emotions rise within my breast,
And surging with a pathos deep,
  Sweep o'er my soul in currents grand,
Whene'er I hear or breathe thy name—
  Sweet Sunny South, my native land!

What other land 'neath Heaven's dome,
  By braver men was ever trod?
What other land on earth is known
  So lavishly endowed by God?
Where else on earth such valorous deeds,
  As by our Southern patriots done;
And where—oh! where—such women true,
  As here beneath our Southern sun?

And in that last great coming morn,
  When God shall bid all sleepers rise
From earth and seas to camps on High,
  Joined hand and heart beyond the skies,
In armistice of eternal peace,
  We'll bivouac then amid the stars,
And reverence, through eternity,
  The stars and stripes and stars and bars!

A man whose noble, chivalrous heart,
  Ne'er hath a pulsing throb
That does not beat for fellow-man,
  For country, and for God.

And till the cycling years of time,
  Have into dark oblivion rolled,
All love of home and native land,
  Their valorous deeds will still be told!

———————

No human tongue, in words, can frame,
  Nor wreath in thoughts, however bright,
The measure of their deathless fame.

———————

Not even that celestial host,
  Who drove with wrathful thunder dire,
The traitor, Satan, and his horde
  From Heaven's courts to pits of fire,
Was more unselfish, brave and true,
  Than was that grand, heroic band,
Who fought beneath the stars and bars,
  For God, for home, and native land!

Ah! there's a poem in her name,
Loved rose of sweetest Southern fame!
In literature's treasure land,
Crowns, gemmed, await her, pen in hand—
E'er filled with jeweled thoughts so grand.

Vain words ne'er find her gifted pen,
Imbued with right, ennobling men;
Vernal spring morns are like her ways—
In angel looks, her beauty sways,
And Virtue's holy smiles (so sweet),
Ne'er leave her fairyland retreat.

Bright one, historian of the heart!
Rich laurel wreaths we bring thy part.
Oh! wield thy brush and pen of love,
While South, the land that's kissed above,
Ne'er loses gems so rare and pure.
Long will thy name and works endure;
Enshrine her art, oh! Southern sky,
Engraft her words where truth can't die!

("FLAMES ON FLINT RIDGE.")

Easier it is to feign what we do not feel, than to
conceal what we do feel.

She had a smile so sweet that it was a pity she
did not smile oftener.

The Lord sweeten the mouth of that feller that
invented the astonishing lie about the trees up
there at Birmingham hanging with old-time frit-
ters, and the lakes full of molasses—nothing to do
but sop, eat, and sleep and wake up and find your
pockets full of dollars, nothing but dollars.

If we could see adown the flight of years,
And know what lies before our way,
We oft would faint before our cares come on,
And have no strength to go on day by day.

The whippowils have the night to themselves
and are filling it with pathos.

Life is like a flowing river:
Men are leaves which on it glide,
Though they strive and e'er endeavor,
They are swept before the tide.

166

("The Affinities.")

Parting, the twin sister of Death, wafts us away on balmy wings.

Heaven designed that woman should reflect beams of cheerfulness and purity upon the broad-spread waste of life.

Casting rays of roseate brilliancy.

What pleases us most does not always make the pot boil.

It was a regular Shadrach, Meshach, and Abed-nego experience.

It will be a constant reminder of the summer days in store for me.

A flirt is a rosebud from which every lover has plucked a petal, leaving the thorn for the future husband.

The air was nectar, the trees marvels of verdure, and the flowers sent out a thousand odors of blended sweetness.

The gold from those dear soft locks has slipped into your heart.

We may speak of men and angels, but the accents of the heart are uttered in a still, small voice and silence is more golden than applause.

He shut up the sweet, sad story of his heart, and guarded it as a miser guards his gold.

He begged to be allowed to insert himself between those he admired most and loved best.

It was a moment never to be forgotten, inexpressibly bitter, yet mingled with a sensation of pleasure so deeply soothing and affecting as at once to awaken and to open the flood-gates of the heart.

Weighed down by a burden heavier and more accursed than ever borne by so honorable a person.

Love you—I have been like a man that has fallen in love with a star, and because it was so far above him he prayed for death if that might bring him nearer it.

———

A silence more eloquent than language.

———

It was told with the quiet conviction of one who utters an eternal truth.

———

Hidden in one of the world's Plebian corners.

———

All regret was sweetened by a dreamy hint of summer days, the future held in store. Within her mind she faintly heard the refrain of a poem whose mystic, passionate lines were born of the mocking birds song and the perfume of flowers.

———

Night spread her pitying wings more closely around the scene; while beneath the throbbing stars the flowers bent their heads in sorrow under the trembling kiss of the dewdrop.

Never did a soldier obey the orders of his commander more willingly than they did the mandates of a guardian angel that had come, sweet as the tinkling of fairy bells, breathing the soul-inspiring word—hope.

If we could only begin life with the experience that is beat into us before its close, what a world of mistakes and troubles would be avoided!

A seventh heaven of delightful expectancy.

Oh! blessed sunlight that enwrapped them as they stood there covered with that light which was never "on sea or on land." They had entered into a realm where they measured not their wealth by acres, nor counted it down in real gold.

This thought, like one draught in the wilderness, was to be refreshment to her heart during the long waste of life before her.

Envy, the incurable cancer of the soul, like the deadly upas tree, destroys with its noxious breath every fair flower that would bloom in the human heart.

12

Nothing can doom us to a life of misery on earth if we have a quickened conscience and follow its dictates.

If we look up we will find radiant stars of cheer and comfort twinkling in the sky of existence.

A melancholy mind imparts a gloomy tinge to everything around it.

No tender wife will ever twine loving arms around my neck and shed tears of sympathy, or illumine my path with her smiles.

Would not vows which rob people of their peace and becloud their hope of heaven be better broken than kept?

It is a grand nature to lose sight of self and become interested in the aspirations of others.

The kind things said of us are life's sunshine.

I trust you will cease to regard as an enemy the one person in all the world who is most anxious to befriend you.

Any and all honest labor that will contribute to my comfort will be honest and sweet to me.

She unconsciously scatters rose leaves and balm plants in the paths of all with whom she comes in contact.

You have that in your face which authorizes trust.

Within the sacred empire of the soul.

Charity! charity! where have you hidden your beautiful face in these days of almighty·dollars?

What a magnificent mind! intuitively correct like a woman's, but competent of reasoning like a man's. Loving, tender, and true, yet capable of stern justice.

Follow the banner of the good knight—sincerity.

Rich legacy of Southern trust!
Untiring work has kept from dust
Both name and thoughts from her so bright—
Young master of the pen of might.

Bold warrior for the Southern pen!
Each plan is voiced and caught again
'Round Dixie's clime, and soon 'twill tell.
Yield long, cute verse, and books as well,
Loved one, proud Birmingham's sweet belle.

Keep watching, South, thy rising star,
Your hopes of such rare genius are;
Long treasure works of her bright name,
Enroll her on the scroll of Fame.

("PAUL ST. PAUL.")

Pale cameo streams wandered from the mother heart of sunset coloring, and through their film, stars gleamed like rose diamonds.

———

She aspires to be a second Dickens and her characters are hollow shells without the echo of the sea.

———

Surprises are the sparkle of existence.

———

Made of themselves serfs to attend her smiles and wishes.

———

They sat all absorbed in the sweet intercourse of spoken love.

———

God keep you pure and sinless, sweet child, and give you death rather than dishonor.

———

Centuries, cycles, milleniums, and eons weigh down this time-worn globe; and yet love never tires of rehearsing her many tragic plays in the sphere of human hearts.

Her calm, sweet smile descended like a benediction upon his wild unrest.

———————

Love, with the velvet sheen of its divinity, half vanished in pale language.

———————

In her heart was a living grave, enshrining a living corpse.

———————

Virtue which thrives in questionable places beggars words for description. It is as white as the ivory battlements around the throne of God. No star is half so pure. It is Heaven incarnated in an earthly mould.

———————

Love means the enslaving of the talents which make men famous.

———————

Make the gift sweet with a smile.

———————

What right had pale day to chalk the tresses of jet and throw drops of languor into those lustrous orbs.

The weeping willows were at their eternal prayers.

———

Not a single jewel marred the gorgeous simplicity of her attire.

———

A veil of satiny, yellow hair, that mocked the very hues of gold, wreathed the slender form in a shroud of sunshine; the face was as fair as one of Raphael's dreaming angels; twin stars, having lost their way in the Heavens had taken refuge underneath snowy lids, and a ruby had left its blood upon her lips.

———

The marble fragments of other days had been for years stowed away in the dead-veined hollows of the past.

———

It was summer in her heart though winter winds raged fearlessly across the bare breast of groaning earth.

———

The ashes of the seared years that were gone fell from the fender.

The ravishing airs from the first violin of God's heavenly orchestra, whose pathos shakes the very pillars of the spheres, were not loud enough to penetrate the icy rind of his soul.

———

Wild rich curls of jet clustered above a high Grecian brow and watched the midnight glow of splendid eyes; soul-deep eyes of darkest night in whose fathomless depths slumbered Promethean fires.

———

Silently memory turned the leaves of life's brilliant book, traversing complacently the shining isles of the dear dead past. The year now fast slipping through Time's greedy fingers was rife with pleasure for him and full of Ambition's dearest consummation—Success. Fame, fickle goddess, had remained steadfast by his side through the vicissitudes of an uncertain career.

———

I loved her so much until it seemed that such a passion could not have been the growth of a lifetime. I knew her in another world and loved her there almost as dearly as in this.

———

The ice-bound years had lusted for the peach-bloom on the cheek of memory.

A tear which did honor to strong manhood, trembled on his cheek.

We have succeeded admirably in wasting a half hour.

He was being refined in the crucible into which destiny casts a man whenever it wishes to make a scoundrel or a demi-god.

Sorrow is the great lapidary who is constantly employed in polishing and refining the soul. Trouble embalms virtue in strong minds.

To forget often means to remember. To be faithless often means to be true.

Never while I have the heart to appreciate and the soul to pray for you, shall I forget your goodness to me.

Too much learning in a lady's composition is as unpardonable as a waste of sugar and spice in a chicken pie.

He was going through one of those terrible
trials from which the weak come forth infamous
and the strong sublime.

Pity in a woman is queen of every emotion.

The eyes were fixed in a dreamy content.

The stars had been sifted from the chariot
wheels of night, all over the higher meadow, and
the moon was leading the milky way in a minuet
along the sky.

Dian beautiful? Her fair face glowed like a
ruby in the sun; brunette night had poured her
ink upon the head of her loveliest votary; and
growing fonder still, emptied the bottle into the
eyes of her mistress.

Ordained of fame and loved of earth,
    And then of Heaven's choosing,
There is no grander, sweeter dream—
    No higher, dearer, better theme
Than Heaven gained; through ego losing.

Are Southland's lilies turned to verse,
Bound fondly in a language terse.

Mock-birds no sweeter songs can sing—
Each poem thrills with patriot-ring:
E'er will "Songs of the South" be known,—
Keepsake of each proud Southern home.

("Songs and Poems of the South.")

The homes of Alabama,
  How beautiful they rise
Throughout her queenly quiet realm,
  Beneath her smiling skies!
The richest odors fill the breeze,
  Her valleys teem with wealth,
And the homes of Alabama
  Are the rosy homes of health.

Oh, come to the South,
The shrine of the sun,
And dwell in its homes,
Sweet, beautiful one!

———

Girl of the Sunny South,
Bright, round thy rosy mouth,
  Dimples and smiles are at play ;
Sweet in thy fountain eyes,
Mirrored, the azure skies,
  Tell us of angels and Heaven alway.

———

Then pledge to-night their memories bright,
  Our noble Southern mothers!
Who in the strife—maid, mother, wife—
  Stood by their sons and brothers!

———

And the locks that swing back, as she swings in
    the breeze,
Are dark as the raven's wing, seen through the
    trees;
The bloom of the peach on her round cheek is
    spread;
Her lips, half apart, dim the holly's pure red;
And her eyes, flashing wildly when with gladness
    they shine,
Have the dark liquid glow of the ripe muscadine.

Voluptuous spring! in this soft Southern clime,
With prodigality of birds and flowers;

Droop down thy willows, Southern land!
　Thy bard, thine orator, is dead.
He sleeps where broad magnolias stand,
　With "summer roses" o'er his head;
The lordly river, sweeping by,
　Curves round his grave, with solemn sigh;
And from yon twinkling orange stem,
The mock-bird pours his requiem!
　Bard of the South! the "Summer Rose"
May perish with the "Autumn Leaf;"
　The footprints left on Tampa's shores,
May vanish with a date as brief;
　But thine shall be the life of fame,
　No winter winds can wreck thy name,
And future minstrels shall rehearse
Thy virtues in memorial verse!

Most rare and beautiful your rhymes!
Arrayed in noble, tender thought,
Rich melody of music chimes
Your airs, in graceful sweetness fraught.

When fame descends from mountain heights,
Around which brilliant star-souls shine,
Rewarding unpretentious lights,
Enwreathed will be the verse of thine.

We looked upon the sky and earth,
    And all did seem so fair
We wondered that so bright a place
    Could be the home of care.
The music of the running brook,
    We fashioned into song;
And gathered whispers from the winds
    To bear its notes along.

And pity 'tis that hearts should learn—
Such trusting hearts as ours—
That sin and sorrow left their blight
Upon earth's fairest flowers.

———

When nature in a merry mood,
Is singing her own praises—
When every dainty dimpled dell
Laughs with its wealth of daisies;
When all the bright-eyed flowers seem
To smile in baby wonder,
And fling their kisses to the breeze,
And nod, and gravely ponder;
When all the little stars that blink
In heaven's blue above us,
Are telling in their own sweet way,
How very much they love us—
And every smiling face we meet
Is true as Heaven meant it—
Oh, is it but reflected light,
Or was it God that sent it?

———

Her life untrammeled by the arts
Of fashion's busy whirl,—
Though portionless and little known,
Give me the country girl!

(St. Augustine.)

In the dreamy land of summer,
  Where sweet nature ever smiles,
Where her laughing face is dimpled,
  With a thousand sunlit skies;
Where the voice of ocean's ever
  Freighted with a wealth of sighs,
And the tall palmetto's creeping
  Nearer to the bending skies;
In that land of song and story,
  Rich with legendary lore,—
Like a ghost of the departed,
  Seems that ancient town of yore,
Pointing with historic fingers
Where the dust of ages lingers.

FROM MRS. ZULA B. COOK'S WRITINGS.

Each goodly deed forms a strong link which the Trusty Guide is forming to draw us to the Mount of Love and Peace.

Disentomb your mind from the earth of illiteracy, cleanse it daily with brush of studious application, and soon its natural sagacities will ascend by successive grades into the brightest elements of refinement.

Why endeavor to avenge the maltreatment of any, when silence manifests an indifferent superiority nobler far than open revenge.

Modesty is a canopy under which every woman should walk who would escape the scorching rays of criticism.

I've a fault to match yours and I cease to com-
  plain.
I would like to remove each incision of pain;
I am ready to come, won't you meet me half way?
When you're guilty of wrong, aren't you willing to
  pay?

13

A blissful marriage is a dipthong uniting two human vowels into one syllable of accord.

Do unkind words befall where compassion should
    win?
Are your deeds sweet with justness or bitter with
    sin?
Do your hands meekly toil or impatiently stay?
Do your feet walk aright or oft lead astray?

No power on earth can recall the spirit of virtue on wing.

The fairest life scene, the truest life-tie
About the old home unceasingly lie;
No grief half so mild, no pleasure so great,
As viewing old home in permanent state.

Sweet are those lips which speak no ill,
And every heart-moan seek to still;
With kisses deep, and whisp'rings soft,
They bring to us earth-glories oft.
God bless them—would all life were blest
With loving lips and love-calm rest.

A young face is the asterism of a happy home life.

Love is the axis on which the wheels of purest
life revolve.

Recognizing questionable character is equal to
an open ballot of approval.

Keep the rifts from your heart, keep it ever apart
From the chis'ling and boring of hate;
With disruption well stayed no repairs can be made,
And you'll never be sighing "too late."

(FAILURE.)

Shall I crouch beneath the weaponed monster?
Shall I shed my heart's blood for his greed?
Shall I clasp my hands and poise then upward,
Plead surrender that I may be freed?
Tho' his dagger-blade may pierce my bosom
Thrice—yea, thrice again—I'll struggling rise!
Failure? No. With courage now I'll journey,
Upward, battling to the victor's skies.

Deep midnight tears, dark midnight tears!
Oh! how the heart quails 'neath its sears!
None seeth save that Wakeful Eye;
Or heareth e'er the pain-wrung sigh.
He only lifts our lashing fears—
Bids comfort follow midnight tears.

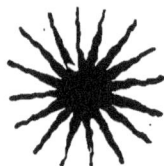

FROM "WAYSIDE GLEANINGS."

BY MRS. FRANCIS JANSENIUS.

Of all things beautiful and grand,
If I could a choice be given,
Let music charm me last on earth
And greet my spirit first in Heaven.

Beneath thy darksome waters safely keep
The many treasures of the mighty deep;
We love thy ceaseless, changing, wild unrest;
Thy peaceful calm or foaming ocean crest.
Majestic, grand, and awful in thy powers we
    know,
Yet enchanting, beauteous Gulf of Mexico!

The advice I would give is to do as you please;
Your mind, if you have one, will feel more at ease,
But expect at each turn to meet all kinds of scandal,
And if you try to stop them you're soon in a tangle,
    For people most surely will talk.

The dream is past, I grieve no more,
    Each tender thought of you has fled;
Not all the wealth of India's mines,
    Would tempt me now with you to wed.

My every day and hour of life
I lived for you and you alone,
And in my sacred heart of hearts,
You dwelt as king upon a throne.

We sat beneath a lofty pine
After a sultry summer day,
Cupid sat listening overhead
To hear what lovers had to say:
He will not tell, and so you see
That talk was just for him and me.
Heart spoke to heart that dewy eve
In language tongue cannot express;
He sought a promise which I gave,
He sealed it with a warm caress!
Cupid approved, and so you see
That love was just for him and me.

Life is like a weary waiting
For a day that never dawns,
When our hearts will be contented
And all vexing cares be gone.

Poetry should be such as to call forth the purest,
holiest thoughts and highest aspirations of the
soul and harmonize with the purest, tenderest
chords of our natures.

Even the sad events of life are brightened when
set to the flow of a pleasant rhyme.

FROM "SONGS OF THE SOUTH."

BY MISS MARY GORDON DUFFEE.

Lone and low in the South, like a star in the
Heavens above,
The orange hangs in a glory of gold on the trees.

———

A land where summer sleeps in the shade of the
palm.

———

Come not with your harp to awaken a hope that
is fled.

———

They list to the music of Heaven; we, only to
strains of regret.

———

The waves flow on, as the heartless world, when a
soul goes down.

———

I'll think of thee in every hour
I pass the lonely spot,
Where Earth wears on her breast the flower
They call Forget-me-not.

You talk of the fragrance of flowers, the beauty
of skies overhead;
Do the roses carven on marble, so pure and so fair,
Yield unto the heart that bends over them the perfume of hope that is fled?
Better dream of the days that await us, the bud
and the bloom over there!

———————

I shall walk in the shadows, down the lonely land
of regret.

———————

Fond memory wove a magic spell
Of other scenes and other years,
Of those who loved us, and who left
Us—parted in the realm of tears.

———————

The night that domes our Southern sky,
Reflects its image in thine eye,
And love breathes in thy tender sigh,
Sweet rose of Alabama!

BY MRS. ALICE KATE ROLAND.

As there are lights and shades in the clouds, and tints and hues belonging to the landscape, which no artist has ever found coloring to portray, so there are heart-sorrows which no pen, however eloquent, has ever described.

———————

The human heart can no more live without love, than the flowers without the refreshing raindrops.

———————

It is for the sake of being pleasing to you that I would look beautiful.

———————

The room was a poem within itself, combining the harmonies of both arrangement and design.

———————

To know you better would be to realize the dearest wish of my life.

———————

Films of white frost mantled the trees with a crystal armor.

In the sullen noise of the waves, an answering voice would speak to me in deep tones, lulling me into a calm content.

Thus we spent many such happy, idle hours, and time fled with the rapidity it displays when no important event occurs to mark its course, and each day being so full of tranquility, that we forgot to look forward or backward.

A low breeze sang among the branches, like a harp accompaniment to the songs of birds.

The poor woman looked the thoughts she could not speak.

Their bright eyes and flower-like lips vied with the flashing gems and blushing roses, with which they were adorned.

It mattered not how I was occupied, there floated before my mental vision a fair face, whose features were of the most exquisite moulding, and whose head was covered with a wealth of dusky, golden hair.

If it be only a bird's nest or an Arab's tent in the desert, there is no place like home.

It is when we are glad that we want the day; but when pain-struck and weary, we ask only for some place in which to hide—somewhere that the soul can slip for a while the restraints of the body and stand face to face with itself. Long ago in compassionate pre-knowledge of this, the dear sympathizing God said: "Let there be night as well as day," and since then into the sympathetic ear of the dark, have been sobbed the secrets of all the restless and grief-laden of earth.

All that we know or feel or breathe of agony is found in the death of those we truly love. Words may express *thoughts* but *feelings never*.

Each heart keeps its diary and in it are pages turned down and blotted with tears for dear remembered dead.

When strains of lovely music die away, they must go to Heaven.

When we receive our slight cuts and bruises in life there is generally an outcry and plenty of sympathy. But when we receive our deep wounds —those that leave scars—often only God knows; and is it not best? For He can *heal*, while our best friends can only *probe*.

The heart cannot relinquish its habits half as readily as the mind.

For every one that sits idle and lets the world go by, there is a burden-bearer who assumes the duties and responsibilities which the rightful owner shirks.

Thoughtlessness is no excuse for a creature endowed with a brain and a heart.

We should not endeavor to purify and make better our lives because, coward-like, we are afraid to displease God, but because He loves us and has redeemed us with an immeasurable demonstration of this love.

'Tis not a human's lot below
To anchor all his ships afar
Within Fruition's vale; and so
    I grieve not when they sink, but know
    Them in thy care, my Guiding Star.

Misfortune may weight the spirit
    That's bound in narrow spheres;
But the one of real merit
    Will rise above his cares.

The cares that try our souls below,
    In mercy sweet are given,
That we may overcome and know
    Them stepping-stones to Heaven.
And sweet it is to sit and dream,
    Amid earth's sunset glare,
Of home beyond the icy stream,
    I shall inherit there,
Beyond the bars—
    Beyond the glorious sunset bars.
This nether-sun I know some day,
    Into the west will fade
To rise again no more for aye,
    In brilliant light arrayed;

I am so weak and small, and yet
When suns have ceased to shine
    And moons and stars for aye have set,
Eternity is mine—
    Beyond the bars—
Beyond the widening sunset bars.

———— ——

Whatever is, is well; there are no flaws
    To mar the great eternal plan,
By which all things are subject to the laws
    That mould the destiny of man.

———————

'Tis well we cannot walk the way alone
    And all our hope is borrowed might;
Would we could blindly trust the Stronger One,
    And know whatever is, is right.

———————

Oh, happy he who ever does his best
    In all the paths of rugged ways!
He knows no sting regret but peace and rest
    In consciousness of well-spent days.

In the silence and the grandeur
  Of a midnight all alone,
Tread I in the sweet illusion
  That the past is back again.
Oh! the Angels of the by-gones,
  Hold a charm for souls contrite,
Though the night be clothed in shadows
  And the spirits walk in white.

To-day in graves in distant land,
  While fame her watch doth keep,
Untended by a kindred hand,
  Some fallen heroes sleep.
And through the coming tide of years,
  Where rest the gallant dead,
Will woman's tribute—flow'rs and tears,
  Bedeck their lonely bed.
Where laurels bloom and ivies twine,
  And winds sigh sad refrain;
Where moan the cypress and the pine,
  Lie some in battle slain;
Sleep on ye noble sainted dead!
  High on the scroll of fame,
(Tho' marble shaft ne'er mark your bed)
  Will be each hero's name!

———

In this sinful world of woes
  Things are all not what they seem;
Oft beneath the surface flows
  Sorrow's dark and turbid stream.

Then let's rejoice with trembling hope,
"Take life as life is given"—
Our sorrows here the gate may ope
That leads the way to Heaven.

Summer flowers twice have come,
With sweet offerings for his tomb;
Autumn winds, with solemn round,
Twice have strewn the leaves around,
And Winter, with his ice-bound clasp,
Twice has come, like Death's cold grasp;
And yet we know no gentle Spring,
To us again our loved will bring!

BY DR. J. M. P. OTTS.

The secret of success consists in the wisdom that discovers the mistakes of to-day, and corrects them in the work of to-morrow.

———

A good woman is an angel without wings. She does not fly from men, but walks with them, and leads them to good.

———

Every man has his peculiarities. A man without peculiarities would be the most peculiar of men.

———

Fools hate the good man who seeks their good, and love the flatterer who seeks their goods.

———

Some speak evil of others as a kind of indirect self-praise.

14

The reason that some give so little to send the gospel to others is because they get so little of it themselves.

———

It is the highest form of originality to say what everybody knows, and yet something that nobody ever said before.

———

Nobody admires the man of many words; everybody loves the man of his word.

———

When men come to believe that there is no goodness on earth, they will soon begin to fancy that there is no God in heaven.

.

———

It is much easier to love the negro when he is a thousand miles away, than when he is your next door neighbor.

Thought is the sap of life, love its flower, and action its fruit.

———————

When Columbus discovered the Orinoco River, he said: "No such river as this can flow from an island. Such a stream must drain the water of a continent." Considering what the Bible is and what it has done for the world, one must say: "No such book as this can flow from the mind of man; it must be a stream that issues from the fountain of divine wisdom and love.

PARTING WORDS.

My kind, dear reader, the time has come for us to say *au revoir*. I sincerely trust that some of these "Echoes" from my heart, through the reverberations of sympathy, have caused, at least, some low re-echoes of kindness, tenderness, aspiration, nobleness, and love from your own heart, all having a tendency to rekindle the flames of love, start the sparks of hope flying heavenward, soothe life, and ennoble the soul.

May the excelsior whispers of your better soul tell you:

> "It is not all of life to live,
> Nor all of death to die;"

And

> "Lives of great men all remind us,
> We can make *our* lives sublime."

May the voice of hope cheer you, may the calm of love soothe you, may the consciousness of virtue ennoble you, may the word of God guide you, and may the blood of Christ redeem you.

And now, kind friend, if our paths through life are so widely separated that we can never meet and exchange the warm grasp of friendship, may we both so live that after our life-work is ended, we can meet on the balmy shores of the Sweet Beyond.